JAN

A BREATH OF FRENCH AIR

NICE   FRANCE

JAN

A BREATH OF FRENCH AIR

NICE   FRANCE

JAN HENDRIK VAN DER WESTHUIZEN

JAN..9
Boulangerie..17
Amuse-bouche..43
Marchand des quatre-saisons.................67
Boucherie..91
Poissonnerie..113
Fromagerie..133
Pâtisserie..145
Mignardise..175
L'Equipe..201
Après minuit..227
Mise en place..247
Index..254

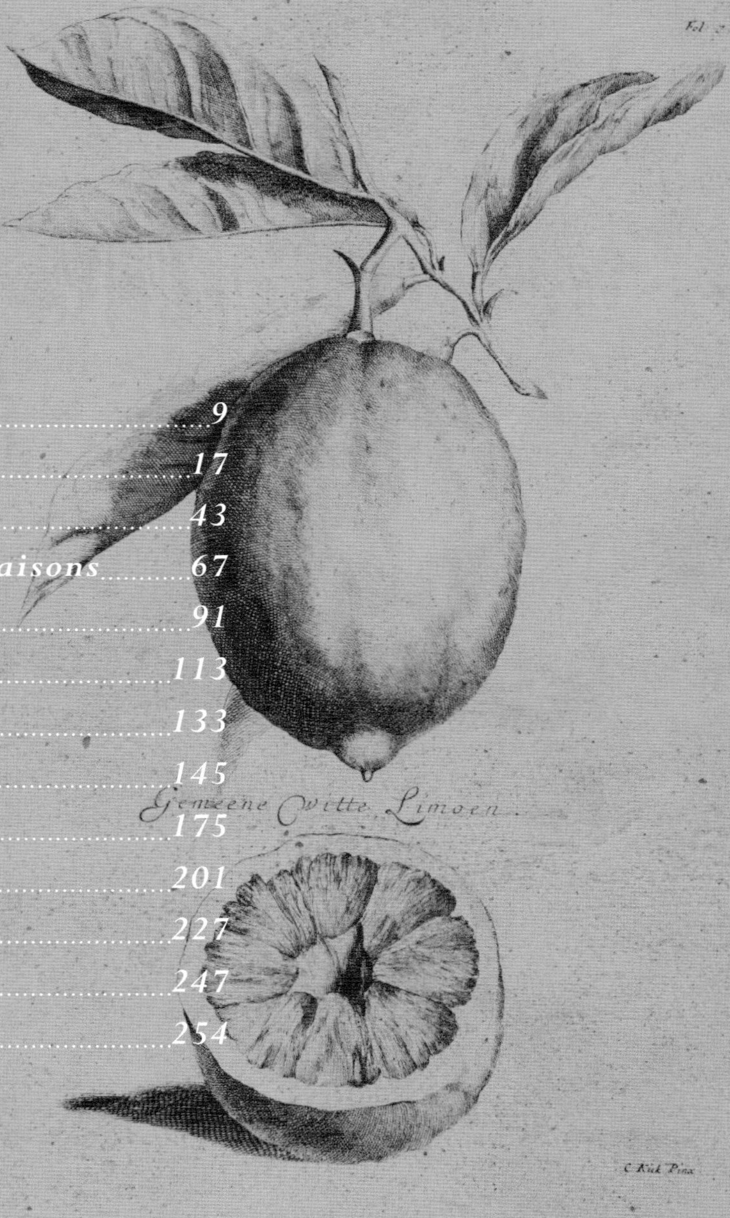

Gemeene Witte Limoen

Fol. 2

C. Risk Pinx

1.

JAN

Every story has a beginning. Mine started at the tables of my mother and grandmother, where the notion of true South African hospitality seeped into my consciousness to become the foundation on which I would later build JAN. It is here that I learned the humble art of serving and creating a warm, welcoming space where people would feel special and escape the humdrum of everyday life, to enjoy the singular pleasures of good company and delicious food.

I've wanted my own restaurant for as long as I can remember. During my time as a student chef, I used to work as a waiter at a commercial family-style steakhouse in a shopping mall with tinny music and fluorescent lighting. This, however, did not deter me from treating the guests at my four tables as though they were seated at the *table grande* at a restaurant in the heart of Paris. Eager to imbue their experience with a sense of occasion, I'd cobble together an *amuse-bouche* from bits and bobs I could gather from the grill and salad bar and serve it very grandly on a slightly chipped saucer.

The story of how this eager young South African lad came to own a restaurant in Nice, France, is one filled with many obstacles, hard work, determination and more than a little bit of luck. I believe that each of us will experience a few occasions in our lives where the stars are perfectly aligned to make our dreams come true. Destiny will shove you into the right place at the right time, but in that moment it remains your responsibility to take the plunge – to close your eyes, leave the safety of your comfort zone and prove how badly you want it, even though you doubt yourself every step of the way.

I still remember clearly the day I told Pascal that I wanted to open a restaurant in France. I was finally ready to run my own kitchen; to leave my mark on each plate of food served. In hindsight, tackling the challenge of feeding the fussy French and battling the red tape that comes with opening a restaurant in France seems like an insurmountable fool's errand. Yet, somehow we managed to pull it off, even with the odds stacked against us.

The day I found the premises, which used to be a motorcycle repair shop, I could envisage it filled to the rafters with contented diners, the rhythmic sound of cutlery against crockery mingling with soothing music. And so our fate was sealed. We enlisted the help of a good friend to assist with the architectural renovations and started our foray into the trying world of doing business with the French, whose relaxed attitude about life extends to construction deadlines. The restaurant's opening date eventually had to be pushed out by a month, but we persevered. Even when our maître d'hôtel, whose previous employers included the five-star La Reserve and London Savoy, arrived and loudly observed that he couldn't visualise the premises as a restaurant.

If anything, we were even more determined to show the native French a thing or two about South African resilience. I attended French classes five days a week, published my first book and shed a few nervous kilograms, all while testing recipes

alongside my newly appointed kitchen staff in a kitchen that had to be washed down four times a day to get rid of dusty layers of powdered chalk. Pascal and I spent innumerable hours with the architect, plumber, electrician, kitchen and service staff to achieve our vision, and the doors of JAN finally opened to the curious French public on a Saturday evening.

We were fully booked and, as things are wont to go when you are essentially living a comedy of errors, the power failed most spectacularly right in the middle of service when we hadn't even started on the main courses for half of the diners. In this type of situation there is only one thing you can do: drink a shot of your dad's homemade *mampoer* (moonshine), offer your guests complimentary Champagne, take a deep breath and regroup. We somehow managed to survive that night and every night since.

Days turned into weeks, months and eventually years, and JAN remains one of my greatest accomplishments and life lessons. Today I manage staff members from all over the world and see to it that the standard of our service and cuisine meets and exceeds the early endeavours that won us numerous awards and prestigious listings. JAN is my homage to South Africa's proud tradition of indiscriminate hospitality, and I'm reminded of my roots every time I pour a glass of Pinotage or serve a plate of food.

I have learned that life rewards you when you live your dream. Go out and find your bliss.

Jan Hendrik

2.

BOULANGERIE

[boo-lanzhuh-ree] a bakery that specialises in baking and selling bread. Masculine *boulanger* (plural *boulangers*, feminine *boulangère*)

Months before we opened the doors to JAN, it was already decided that we would bake our own bread. Throughout the storms that waged in the lead-up to opening day, I would calm myself by imagining patrons sitting down to the alluring aroma of our freshly baked bread.

In my mind's eye I could see them sipping wine and breaking off pieces of warm, light bread with a perfectly crisp crust, slathering it in a thick layer of salted butter or using it to mop up a silky sauce.

For me, the smell of fresh bread is the smell of life and love. It's in the touch of the dough and the warm, yeasty smell that wafts from the oven when you open it to reveal perfectly raised loaves, just waiting to be glazed or lovingly dusted in flour.

I still remember the day a French boulanger spoke to me about his craft. He spoke with such passion and enthusiasm, his great hands flying about like a conductor's, scattering leftover flour that gently sifted down in the rays of sunlight coming in through a small window in the bakery. From his mouth the specifics of baking — the types of flour, yeast and pre-ferments — sounded like an incantation.

It is this boulanger who told me that when he touches the dough to shape it into his pans, he always gets the feeling that, despite all the bad in the world, everything will be okay. I tend to agree.

BAKE BREAD
LIKE THE FRENCH

GIFT
IDEA

What's the secret?

A pre-ferment is the secret that gives bread its stellar flavour. It is a basic mixture of flour, water and yeast that is left to stand for hours, and is then added to the remaining flour, resulting in the perfect loaf of bread.

I get put off when I read a recipe that takes hours to make, but when it comes to bread there is no real shortcut. And the hours are worth every crumb! Make your own pre-ferment and feed it regularly. There are two basic types we use: a levain for the sourdough breads and a poolish for the baguettes.

Boulangeries also have the privilege of using convection steam ovens. This allows the bread to steam so that it rises fully before a crust forms. To create your own steam, heat a skillet in the bottom of your oven and add ice cubes when you put the bread into the oven. Be careful not to burn yourself as the steam can be vigorous.

LEVAIN

250 g strong flour or bread flour
250 ml water

Combine the flour and water with a fork in a plastic container. Cover with plastic wrap and make holes in the plastic. Let it sit for 24 hours in a warm place in your kitchen (at JAN we put it on our pastry fridge).

Now feed the levain on a daily basis (twice if possible) by making a new batch of flour and water mix (same as above), then add 150 g of the old mixture to the new one. Mix well and allow to rest for 12 hours before repeating the process.

Feeding the levain regularly means that you will throw away a lot of the starter, but there's unfortunately no other way until you have reached the right consistency and the levain forms little bubbles. Don't throw the extra levain down the drain, as gluten is not water-soluble. Rather dispose of it in the garbage can. After 2–3 days of feeding, the leftover levain will get used in your daily bread preparation. It does sound a bit complicated, but the moment you're into it, it's kind of addictive!

STIFF LEVAIN

350 g strong flour or bread flour
170 ml water
30 g levain (see left)

Mix all the ingredients together, cover loosely with plastic wrap and allow to rest for at least 12 hours before using.

POOLISH

150 g flour
Pinch instant yeast
150 ml lukewarm water (at 25 °C)

Combine the flour and yeast in a bowl and mix well with your fingers. Add the water and combine – the dough should be runny. Cover loosely with plastic wrap and allow to rest at room temperature for about 12 hours. Bubbles will form and a thin crust will indicate when it's ready to use.

BAGUETTES

Makes: *4*

Difficulty: *Little effort*

Prep time: *25 min +*
2 hr 45 min proving (excl
making the poolish in advance)

Baking time: *25–30 min*

INGREDIENTS

1 batch Poolish (see page 18)

400 g strong flour or white bread
flour, plus extra

1 sachet (10 g) instant dry yeast

260 ml lukewarm water

5 ml fine sea salt

METHOD

Prepare the poolish in advance. Place the flour and yeast in a stand mixer fitted with the dough hook. Mix the yeast until combined with the flour. Add the poolish and water to the flour and yeast and mix on a low speed for 5 minutes until the dough is hydrated. Scrape down the sides twice during this process. Sprinkle the salt on top and mix for another 20 minutes on low speed. The dough will not be firm and will not form a ball; it should be sticky and slack.

Place the dough into a bowl sprayed with nonstick spray, cover and allow to rest for 1 hour. Gently remove from the bowl and place on a lightly floured surface. The dough will be very sticky. Sticking to your fingers is a good sign. Stretch the dough upwards and outwards and fold it in two-thirds, then stretch it to the opposite side. Repeat one more time, then gently lift with a dough scraper and place into the bowl to rest for another 1 hour.

Repeat the stretch process once more and then rest the dough for the last hour before scraping it onto a floured work surface to cut. Divide the dough into four equal portions and form long shapes. Roll gently with your hands, keeping the seam of the bread at the bottom. The best way to bake the bread is to place it on baker's linen to retain the baguette shape, but you can also use silicone baking sheets. Cover the baguettes with a cloth and allow to prove for about 45 minutes in a warm place.

Preheat the oven to 210 °C and place a skillet in the bottom of the oven. Score the baguettes with a razor – don't cut too deep – then transfer to the oven. Immediately place a few ice cubes in the skillet and close the door. Bake for 25–30 minutes until the bread feels lighter than you expect for the size.

CAPE SEED LOAF

GIFT
IDEA

Makes: *5 loaves*

Difficulty: *Easy*

Prep time: *20 min +*
30 min proving

Baking time: *20–25 min*

The kitchen in Stellenbosch, where I worked as a waiter while studying to be a chef, did a Cape seed loaf to utmost perfection. They were pretty famous for it and I remember how the guests kept asking for more, even wanting to take it home with them. After reworking the recipe, I've found a combination that is both crunchy and soft, very much the way I remember the bread as a student. At JAN, if there are any loaves left over after service, they are wrapped up in brown paper bags for the last few tables to take home or they go home with me to enjoy as a midnight snack.

INGREDIENTS

30 ml sugar

2½ sachets (10 g each) instant dry yeast

760 ml lukewarm water

900 g strong flour or white bread flour

430 g wholewheat flour

110 g flax seeds

55 g sesame seeds

60 ml poppy seeds

110 g honey

90 ml olive oil

30 ml fine sea salt

METHOD

Place the sugar and the yeast in a bowl and add the water. Set aside for about 10 minutes until bubbles start to form.

In the bowl of a stand mixer fitted with the dough hook, add the flours and seeds, and mix on a low speed until well combined. Add the yeast mixture, honey and oil and mix for another 10 minutes until the dough starts coming together. Add the salt and continue mixing for another 10 minutes. The dough will be soft and slightly wet.

Grease five 26 cm x 7 cm loaf tins with nonstick spray. Transfer the dough onto a work surface lightly dusted with flour and flatten to form a square. Cut the dough into equal strips and place gently in the loaf tins. Make sure there are no folds, but if there are, make sure they are tucked underneath. Place in a warm area to prove for 20–30 minutes. Don't overprove as the bread will be too light – I like the little bit of density.

Preheat the oven to 200 °C and bake for 20–25 minutes, or until golden brown. Immediately remove the loaves from the tins (otherwise they will sweat) and place on a cooling rack. (We cover ours with linen cloths so that they are still slightly warm when served.)

FRENCH WHITE BREAD

Makes: *2 loaves*

Difficulty: *Medium*

Prep time: *30 min + 3 hr proving (excl making the levain in advance)*

Baking time: *20–25 min*

INGREDIENTS

12.5 ml active dry yeast

180 ml lukewarm water

Pinch sugar, plus extra 5 ml

110 g levain (see page 18)

500 g strong flour or white bread flour

1 ml bicarbonate of soda

5 ml fine sea salt

Served fresh or toasted with our cheese board, this classic is a staple in JAN's kitchen. To make the perfect melba toast, freeze and slice the loaf with a mandoline before toasting.

METHOD

Use a stand mixer with the dough hook attachment. Using the mixing bowl, dissolve the yeast in the water. Add the pinch of sugar to enhance the activation process. Allow to stand for 10 minutes.

Add the levain, the 5 ml sugar and the flour and mix on a low speed for 10–15 minutes. Cover the bowl with a cloth and let the dough rise for 1–1½ hours. Mix again on low speed for 10 minutes and add the bicarbonate of soda and salt. The dough should be soft in texture and form a ball. If the texture is still sticky, add a little bit of flour. Shape the dough into a ball on a floured surface and let it rest for 10 minutes.

Form two loaves and place on a greased baking tray. Dust lightly with flour and score the dough vertically with a razor blade. Let them prove for 1½ hours.

Preheat the oven to 200 °C and bake for 20–25 minutes, or until light brown.

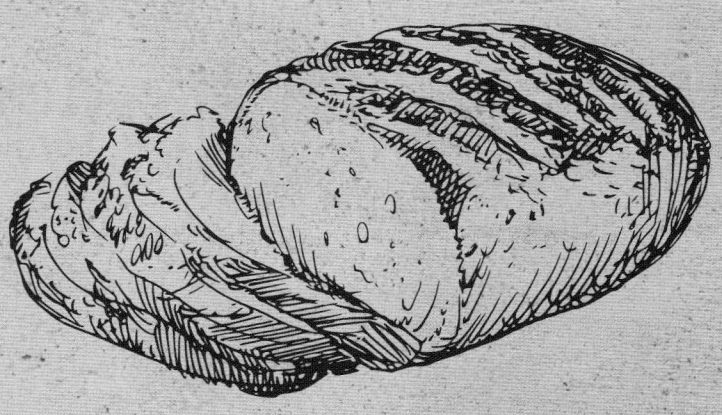

PAIN RUSTIQUE

Makes: *2 loaves*

Difficulty: *Medium*

Prep time: *20 min + 3½ hr proving (excl making the levain in advance)*

Baking time: *30–45 min*

INGREDIENTS

160 g levain (see page 18)

275 ml lukewarm water

300 g strong flour or white bread flour

75 g light rye flour

5 ml fine sea salt

A sweet perfumed crumb and a lovely caramelised crust. Rye flour mixed with white flour results in a rustic texture that is still soft to the touch. This bread is not baked in a tin so can be shaped into whatever form your heart desires.

METHOD

Dissolve the levain in 180 ml of the water in a mixing bowl.

In the bowl of a stand mixer fitted with the dough hook attachment and sprayed with nonstick spray, add the flours and mix on low speed until combined. Add the levain mixture and continue mixing until you get a texture of wet flour coming together. Cover the bowl and let it stand for 20–30 minutes.

After the resting period, add the salt and the rest of the water and mix for 10 minutes on low speed. Transfer the dough to a greased bowl and cover lightly with plastic wrap. Set aside for about 1 hour.

Transfer the dough onto a lightly floured work surface and start the stretch process similar to the baguette recipe (see page 20). Stretch the dough upwards and outwards and fold it in two-thirds. Then stretch it to the opposite side. Rest the dough for 30–40 minutes. Repeat one more time, then gently lift with a dough scraper and place into the bowl to rest for another 1 hour.

After the final rest you need to shape the dough into a *bâtard* or other loaf shape, using light dustings of flour to help you shape the bread. Fold any pleats underneath to get a smooth top. Using a razor blade, score the bread with a few cuts and place on a lightly floured baking tray. Allow to prove, lightly covered, in a warm place for 1–1½ hours.

Preheat the oven to 230 °C and place a skillet in the bottom of the oven. Transfer the loaves to the oven. Immediately place a few ice cubes in the skillet and close the door. Bake for 30–45 minutes until the bread has a golden crust.

PAIN DE MIE

Makes: *2 loaves*
Difficulty: *Medium*
Prep time: *45 min +*
3–4 hr proving
Cooking time: *20–25 min*

We all grew up with a slice of soft white bread with a crumb. Pain de mie literally means soft bread with a crumb and is similar to the ones you can buy at the supermarket. However, to make your own makes you feel much less guilty when enjoying it piled with fresh tomatoes, cheese and thinly sliced onion. Actually, why should we feel guilty? At JAN we make pain de mie only on special occasions — perhaps when there is too much levain or if there is time to add a loaf or two to the rest of the bread in the oven.

INGREDIENTS

7.5 ml instant dry yeast
550 g all-purpose flour
20 ml sugar
7.5 ml fine sea salt
280 g lukewarm water
1 medium-sized egg, beaten
30 ml unsalted butter, melted
80 g cream cheese

METHOD

Spray the bowl of a stand mixer fitted with a dough hook, as well as two loaf tins, with nonstick spray.

Place the yeast and flour in the bowl and mix on low for a few minutes. Combine the sugar, salt, water, egg and butter and mix for a further 10 minutes. Add the cream cheese and mix for 20 minutes. Cover with a cloth and allow to rest for 15 minutes.

Turn out the dough onto a floured work surface. Flatten the dough and stretch the points towards each other and then flatten again. Repeat twice. Cover and allow to rest for another 15 minutes.

Flatten the dough into a rectangular shape, adding flour to prevent it from sticking to the surface. Cut the dough into two 500 g portions. Shape the dough as much as possible into the shape of the pan. Place the dough gently in the pans and cover to proof for 2–3 hours.

Preheat the oven to 200 °C. Bake for 20–25 minutes on the lower rack of the oven — a proper *pain de mie* loaf tin has a lid, so use it if you have one (but it's also okay to bake it without a lid). Test the bread with a needle, which should come out clean when the bread is baked.

PRETZELS WITH KALAHARI DESERT SALT

Makes: *20 medium-sized pretzels*
Difficulty: *Little effort*
Prep time: *15 min + overnight proving (excl making the levain in advance)*
Baking time: *25 min*

INGREDIENTS

Levain Starter
1 batch stiff levain (see page 18)

Pretzels
950 g strong flour or bread flour
1 sachet (10 g) instant dry yeast
30 ml fine sea salt
490 ml lukewarm water
120 g butter, melted

Dipping liquid
30 ml sodium hydroxide (lye)
500 ml water

Kalahari Desert salt or Maldon salt (half a pinch per pretzel)

A common story tells us that these soft, salty strips of dough, folded in the shape of a child in prayer, originated around AD 610 by an Italian monk. Other similar stories star a monk from France and bakers held hostage in Germany. Whatever the origin, these knots never fail to please. This recipe calls for sodium hydroxide, which gives the pretzel its hard skin and terrific colour. It can be obtained from your local hardware store and is often used for making soap. When shopping, look for food grade lye; alternatively, you can use bicarbonate of soda or egg wash but it won't give the same crust and flavour. Wear latex gloves and work on sheets cut from large garbage bags.

METHOD

Spray the bowl of a stand mixer with nonstick spray. Combine the flour, yeast and salt in the bowl and mix briefly on the lowest setting. Add the stiff levain, water and butter and mix for 5 minutes. Mix for another 25 minutes until a soft dough forms. Turn out onto a work surface lightly dusted with flour, then stretch the dough by pulling all the points away and then back towards the centre. Fold the dough in half and repeat the stretching process. Cover with plastic wrap and let it stand for 15 minutes.

Place the dough onto the floured work surface again and add more flour to prevent it from sticking. Divide the dough into small balls and roll them with both hands into a breadstick shape. Now fold the two points downwards making a circle shape and then take the points back up, crossing each other, and press down on the top part of the circle. Arrange about six pretzels per baking tray and refrigerate, uncovered, for 2 hours until they form a skin.

Meanwhile, prepare the dipping liquid by carefully adding the sodium hydroxide to the water (NB: always add the lye to the water, never the other way around) and stir with a spoon in a big stainless-steel bowl until the crystals have dissolved. Wearing gloves, dip the pretzels one by one into the mixture and let them soak for about 10 seconds. Shake off the excess liquid carefully and place the pretzels back on the baking tray – do not let them touch.

Preheat the oven to 180 °C. Sprinkle the pretzels with Kalahari or Maldon salt and bake for 25 minutes, or until golden in colour. Cool on a rack before serving.

MOSBOLLETJIES

Makes: *7 'cups' or 2 loaves*
Difficulty: *Medium*
Prep time: *30 min +*
   1 hr proving
Baking time: *25–30 min*

The French locals love this South African bread; it is probably because of the similarity to brioche, to which mosbolletjies owe a small part of their deliciousness. We bake ours in individual copper cups, which I originally bought as cocktail cups for making a Russian mule. So between the French, South Africans and the Russians, we love to watch our guests gently break open the warm mosbolletjie on its seam and dip it into a lemony olive oil from the neighbouring village of Menton.

INGREDIENTS

1 kg all-purpose flour
80 g sugar
1½ sachets (10 g each) instant
   dry yeast
30 ml whole aniseeds
300 ml white grape juice
220 g butter
100 ml lukewarm milk
250 ml lukewarm water
15 ml fine sea salt
Apricot jam for brushing

METHOD

Grease two loaf tins measuring 26 cm x 7 cm or individual tin cups with nonstick spray or melted butter.

In the bowl of a stand mixer fitted with the dough hook, add the flour, sugar, yeast and aniseed, and mix on a low speed until well combined.

Warm the grape juice and stir in the butter until melted. Add this to the flour mixture along with the warm milk and water. Mix on a medium speed for 10 minutes until the dough comes together. Add the salt and mix for another 10 minutes. Remove the dough and place into a greased bowl. Cover lightly with plastic wrap and allow to stand for 20–30 minutes in a warm place until the dough has almost doubled in size.

Knock down the dough, pinch off pieces and shape into balls by pressing and pulling the dough through a circle formed by your other thumb and forefinger. We spray our hands lightly with nonstick spray to prevent the dough from sticking. Squeeze in three balls per cup (or pack the balls tightly into the loaf tin/s).

Place the cups in a warm area to prove for 20–30 minutes (this might take longer depending on the temperature). Make sure the *mosbolletjies* are well proved, as this will without a doubt affect the soft texture.

Preheat the oven to 180 °C and bake for 30 minutes, or until light brown. Remove immediately from the tin cups, otherwise they will sweat. Melt the apricot jam and brush over the heads of the *mosbolletjies*. To serve, place back into the cups after they have cooled completely.

PAIN AU CHOCOLAT

Makes: *24 croissants*
Difficulty: *Little effort*
Prep time: *40 min +*
    4 hr chilling and proving
Baking time: *15–20 min*

INGREDIENTS

6 ml active dry yeast
45 ml lukewarm water
15 ml castor sugar
250 g all-purpose flour
7.5 ml fine sea salt
160 ml warm milk
30 ml vegetable oil
370 g butter
230 g dark chocolate, chopped
  (70% cocoa)
1 medium-sized egg

We don't serve this at JAN, but we do get the best chocolate croissants just around the corner. Lucky us! I used to make these on our farm in South Africa and they were delicous with a cup of moer koffie *(coffee made with ground coffee beans). Some prefer a thin slice of chocolate whereas I go for a big chunk — good quality* bien sûr *(of course)!*

METHOD

Combine the yeast, warm water and 5 ml of the castor sugar in a bowl and allow to stand until creamy and frothy.

Measure the flour into a mixing bowl. Dissolve the remaining 10 ml castor sugar and the salt in the warm milk, then mix into the flour with the yeast mixture and oil. Mix well for about 5 minutes, then knead until smooth. Cover and leave to prove until tripled in volume. Gently press down and then let it rise again until doubled in volume. Press down once more and then refrigerate for 20 minutes.

Remove the butter from the fridge and allow to reach near room temperature, just enough so that it can be flattened out into a rough rectangle of 60 cm x 30 cm.

Roll out the dough into a large rectangle. Place the butter on top of the dough, making sure it covers two-thirds of it. Then fold the third that is not covered with the butter over the butter-covered dough. A third of the butter-covered dough will be exposed. Fold that back onto the dough, layering the dough and the butter. Roll out the butter and dough layers carefully with a rolling pin to compress them. Cover and refrigerate for 15 minutes.

Repeat the folding and chilling process twice more. Cover loosely with plastic wrap and refrigerate for a couple of hours, or overnight.

Roll out the chilled dough into a large rectangle about 1 cm thick. Cut the dough into 12 cm squares using a sharp knife. Cut each square diagonally to create two triangles. Arrange a row of roughly cut chocolate along the long edge of each triangle and roll up the dough to form a sausage shape.

Place the *pain au chocolat* on a baking tray lined with greaseproof paper. Cover with sprayed plastic wrap and leave for 1 hour to prove until puffed up and light.

In a small bowl, beat together the egg and 15 ml water. Glaze the croissants with the egg wash.

Preheat the oven to 220 °C and bake for 15–20 minutes until risen and golden brown. Serve lukewarm.

3.

AMUSE-BOUCHE

[aˌmyzˈbuʃ] (plural *amuse-bouches*) or
amuse-gueule [aˌmyzˈgœl] — mouth amuser

The direct translation of amuse-bouche *is 'mouth amuser', which I think is a great way to describe the small, complimentary hors d'oeuvres offered to diners in French establishments.*

These bite-sized appetisers serve as a glimpse into the chef's approach to the art of cuisine before guests settle in for their meal, and also speak to the true art of hospitality — in an industry that can become quite focused on price, it is often nice to 'amuse' your guests with a little something unexpected. Plus, it is just such a lekker word to say! The bouche *bounces off the tongue in the most delightful way.*

At JAN we serve our amuse-bouche *after the bread plate, which allows our guests to enjoy it alongside an apéritif. The daily offering varies greatly, but normally serves as a departure point for a new dish, which often combines tradition and innovation in true JAN style.*

The portion sizes in this chapter are similar to what we'd prepare for dinner service at JAN, which means it is sufficient for a large party or snazzy event.

PISSALADIÈRE
(A NIÇOISE ONION TART)

Serves: *Average 18 small portions*
Difficulty: *Easy*
Prep time: *1 hr + 1 hr proving*
Cooking time: *15–20 min*

This is traditional street food in Nice, and classic market fare. Although it is sometimes called a Niçoise pizza, the two dishes are not related. It is difficult to get your hands on a good anchovy paste, but this can be substituted with whole anchovy fillets. Alternatively, make your own paste by blending anchovies in a food processor with a dash of olive oil.

INGREDIENTS

Dough

1 sachet (10 g) instant dry yeast
250 ml lukewarm water
60 ml extra virgin olive oil
450 g all-purpose flour
15 ml fine salt
Cornflour for dusting

Topping

60 ml extra virgin olive oil
1 kg yellow onions, peeled and
very thinly sliced
Sea salt
Ground black pepper
Bouquet garni* with 2 sprigs
marjoram and 2 sprigs rosemary
added
Anchovy paste (optional)
60 g small black olives, pitted
12 anchovy fillets

METHOD

To make the dough, dissolve the yeast in the water in a small bowl. Let it stand for 10 minutes and then add the oil. Combine the flour and salt in the bowl of a stand mixer fitted with a dough hook. Add the yeast mixture and mix on low speed until the dough comes together and all the ingredients are well mixed. Add a bit more water if necessary. Turn out the dough onto a lightly floured surface and form into a ball. Place in a lightly oiled bowl and cover with a damp cloth. Allow to rise in a warm place for about 1 hour.

For the topping, heat the oil in a large pan over medium to low heat. Add the onions and season generously with salt and pepper. Add the bouquet garni and cover the pan. Simmer the onions over low heat for 45 minutes, stirring occasionally. The onions should caramelise into a golden marmalade consistency. It will take anything between 40 and 45 minutes. Remove the bouquet garni and discard.

Roll out the dough on a floured surface into a flat rectangle about 7 mm thick. Transfer the dough to a baking tray sprayed with nonstick spray and dusted with cornflour. Cover the dough again with a damp cloth and allow to rest for 30 minutes.

Remove the cloth and spread a thin layer of anchovy paste over the top of the dough. Spread the onions evenly over the anchovy paste. Arrange the olives and anchovy fillets over the onions, then season lightly with pepper.

Preheat the oven to 230 °C and bake for 15–20 minutes until the crust is brown. Cut into squares and serve warm or at room temperature.

* Bouquet garni: A bundle of herbs tied together with a string and usually added to a dish during cooking to add flavour. It is removed before serving. Herbs that can be used include thyme, bay leaf, rosemary, parsley and sage.

FIG AND BLUE CHEESE MINI TARTE TATINS

Serves: *4*
Difficulty: *Easy*
Prep time: *1 hr*
Baking time: *20 min*

INGREDIENTS

4 medium-sized ripe figs

15 ml sugar

15 ml honey

300 g puff pastry

Sea salt

Ground black pepper

160 g Roquefort, fourme d'ambert
*   or any blue cheese, crumbled*

We can't get enough of these little caramelised upside-down fig and blue cheese tarts. They are the perfect snack with a glass of red during the autumn months. Fig trees grow in abundance in the south of France, on every corner and in every neighbour's garden.

METHOD

Cut the ends off the figs and then slice the figs in half horizontally. Melt the sugar and honey with a small dash of water until just starting to caramelise.

Preheat the oven to 180 °C. Cut the puff pastry in 3–4 cm circles and set aside. In small tartlet pans or mini muffin pans that have been sprayed with nonstick spray, pour some caramel on the base and top with half a fig. Season with salt and pepper and then top with the circle of puff pastry. Gently press down and place in the oven. Bake for 20 minutes, or until the puff pastry is golden.

Remove from the oven and allow to rest for 5 minutes. Remove the tatins from the pans and place on an oven tray, pastry side on the bottom. Sprinkle with blue cheese and return to the oven for 5 minutes just before serving to melt the cheese and warm the tarts.

GRILLED PRAWN WITH COURGETTE FLOWER, CUCUMBER AND AVOCADO GAZPACHO

Serves: *12*
Difficulty: *Easy*
Prep time: *30 min + 2 hr chilling*
Cooking time: *5 min*

INGREDIENTS

Gazpacho

2 cucumbers, chilled
250 ml Greek yoghurt
10–15 courgette flowers
3 sprigs fresh dill, plus extra
Juice of 1 lime
250 ml ice water
Sea salt and ground black pepper
1 ripe avocado
10 ml green Tabasco sauce
   (optional)

Prawns

2 cloves garlic
2 cm piece fresh ginger
Zest and juice of 2 lemons
12 large prawns, deveined and
   shelled (keep tails intact)
Sea salt and ground black pepper
15 ml grapeseed oil or olive oil

METHOD

For the gazpacho, halve the cucumbers lengthways and scoop out the seeds. Place one cucumber (keep the other aside for garnish), the Greek yoghurt, courgette flowers (reserve a few for garnish), dill, lime juice, ice water and seasoning in a blender and blend until it liquifies. Refrigerate the gazpacho for at least 2 hours.

For the prawns, chop the garlic and ginger very finely and add the lemon zest and juice. Mix the cleaned prawns in the garlic mixture and season well with salt and pepper. Heat the oil in a saucepan and fry the prawns on both sides until cooked. Be careful not to overcook the prawns; they must still be juicy and tender.

To serve, cut the avocados and reserved cucumber in brunoise* and season lightly with some lime juice, salt and pepper. Pour the gazpacho into bowls and place the cucumber garnish and avocado in the centre with some fresh dill leaves, a courgette flower and some Tabasco. Place a prawn in the middle and serve immediately.

* Brunoise: Finely diced into small cubes.

SOCCA

Serves: *Makes 3–4 (23 cm)*
pancakes
Difficulty: *Easy*
Prep time: *5 min +*
2–3 hr resting
Cooking time: *10 min*

This medieval chickpea flour pancake, which is also called farinata, originated in Genoa, Italy, and is a typical food of the Ligurian sea coast from Pisa to Nice. Served with freshly milled black pepper, they are at their best straight from the oven.

Thereza, a vendor at the Cours Selaya market in Nice, has become an institution in the area. Her husband brings the socca on the back of his modified bicycle while she, dressed to kill, serves wine in plastic cups. Delightful!

INGREDIENTS

150 g chickpea flour
250 ml water
20 ml fine sea salt
pinch ground cumin
60 ml extra virgin olive oil
Ground black pepper

METHOD

In a large bowl, mix the chickpea flour, water, salt and cumin with the olive oil. Whisk until all the ingredients comes together. Allow the batter to rest at room temperature for 2–3 hours, covered.

Preheat the grill in your oven. Place a cast-iron pan under the grill for a few minutes until boiling hot. Remove and pour in just enough batter to cover the bottom of the pan. Give it a swirl and return to the oven. Bake until firm and a bit of burn starts to happen on the top. Remove from the pan and repeat with the rest of the batter.

Slice into pieces and sprinkle with black pepper, salt and a drizzle of olive oil.

WHITE CHOCOLATE AND SCALLOP ICE CREAM WITH CAULIFLOWER PURÉE AND BLACK RICE CHIPS

Serves: *Average 28 small portions*
Difficulty: *Medium*
Prep time: *1 hr*
Cooking time: *25–30 min*

INGREDIENTS

Scallop Ice Cream
500 g fresh scallops
250 ml fresh cream
125 ml melted white chocolate
5 ml green Tabasco sauce
30 ml white balsamic vinegar
Sea salt and ground black pepper

Cauliflower Purée
1½ heads cauliflower, broken into
florets
500 ml fresh cream
30 ml butter
10 ml fine sea salt

Black Rice Chips
200 g basmati rice
500 ml water
Pinch sea salt
10 ml squid ink
1 L canola oil for deep-frying

METHOD

For the ice cream, blend all the ingredients together in a blender for 10 minutes, or until smooth. Strain through a fine-mesh sieve, follow the manufacturer's instructions for your ice-cream machine and churn until smooth.

For the cauliflower purée, place the cauliflower in a large saucepan and cover with the cream. Bring the mixture to a boil over medium to high heat, then reduce the heat to low. Simmer for about 20 minutes until the cauliflower is tender. Drain and reserve the liquid. Melt the butter in a small saucepan and keep on a low to medium heat until the butter has turned brown. Be careful not to burn the butter. Purée the cauliflower in a blender, adding the liquid 15 ml at a time, then add the salt and browned butter. Pass though a fine-mesh sieve and cool immediately on ice. Pour into a plastic squeeze bottle to use later.

To make the rice chips, combine the rice and water in a medium-sized saucepan over medium heat, cover and cook until all the water has evaporated. Remove from the heat and leave covered until the rice is very soft. Place the rice, salt and squid ink in a blender and process until a very smooth paste is formed. Spread the paste very thinly on silicone mats and leave in a warm place to dry completely. Heat the oil to 190 °C in a medium-sized saucepan. Break the rice sheets into small pieces and drop into the oil. Once they have puffed up, remove with a slotted spoon and place on paper towel to drain any excess oil. Season lightly with salt while still hot.

To serve, squeeze some spots of cauliflower purée onto the plate, followed by a quenelle* of ice cream. Break the black rice chips into pieces and arrange randomly. For extra garnish, use pickled Japanese mushrooms and bean sprouts.

* Quenelle: A special shape made by using a dessertspoon. Dip the spoon (the bowl of which will determine the size of the quenelle) in hot water. Hold the spoon with the round bottom facing up and place the far edge into the mixture. Drag the spoon towards you and the mixture should form a curly shape in the spoon. Twist your wrist upwards until the mixture falls into an egg shape. Practice makes perfect!

SOUTTERT WITH SUN-DRIED TOMATO JAM AND CHARROUX MUSTARD

Serves: *28 (cut into small cubes)*
Difficulty: *Easy*
Prep time: *20 min +*
  1 hr 30 min chilling
Cooking time: *25–30 min*

'Quiche!' was the first thing my French sous-chef screamed when he saw the big pan coming from the oven. It is somewhat true… the egg, bacon, cream, butter and the pâte brisée *(shortcrust pastry) are all a direct influence of the French Huguenots who settled in the Cape, but I shook my head and said 'Oh no! This is* souttert! *My mother's* souttert!'

INGREDIENTS

Crust
350 g all-purpose flour
7.5 ml fine salt
Pinch cayenne pepper
7.5 ml baking powder
125 g butter, at room temperature
15 ml granulated sugar

Filling
½ onion or 2 shallots, chopped
250 g bacon, diced
2 eggs, hard-boiled
30 g quality wholegrain mustard
30 g parsley, chopped
30 ml butter
30 ml all-purpose flour
250 ml milk
90 g Comté cheese or strong
  Cheddar, grated

Cream Topping
1 egg
125 ml milk

METHOD

For the crust, mix all the ingredients together in a stand mixer fitted with the whisk, and mix until a crumble texture forms. When you press the crumbles together, it should form a dough. Cover with plastic wrap and refrigerate for 20 minutes.

For the filling, heat a large saucepan and fry the onion and bacon until soft and slightly brown. Transfer to a blender. Reserve the fat left in the pan. Add the boiled eggs, mustard and parsley to the blender and blend until smooth. There should still be little pieces of bacon, which is good for texture. Melt the butter in the same pan with the leftover fat from the bacon and add the flour and salt. Whisk until it forms a smooth paste, then add the milk and whisk continuously until a smooth béchamel is formed. Add the cheese and then the bacon and onion mixture. Stir well with a wooden spoon.

Line a large baking tray with baking paper and spray with nonstick spray. Using your fingers, press the dough onto the bottom of the pan to form a thin, even base. Pour the filling mixture over the base and spread evenly with a ladle. Refrigerate for 15 minutes.

Preheat the oven to 180 °C. For the topping, whisk the egg and milk together and pour over the top of the filling. Bake for 20–25 minutes until golden brown. Once baked, let it cool completely on a cooling rack. Refrigerate for 1 hour to make it easier to cut. Slice the tart into equal, bite-sized squares and serve with the sun-dried tomato jam (see page 252).

SEARED TUNA WITH ASPARAGUS AND WHIPPED EGG YOLK

Serves: *30*

Difficulty: *Easy*

Prep time: *15 min +*
30 min chilling

Cooking time: *1 hr 30 min*

INGREDIENTS

15 ml sesame oil

5 ml English mustard

500 g sashimi-quality tuna fillet,
cut into logs of an even thickness
and length

60 ml black peppercorns, crushed
roughly

200 g fresh asparagus

50 ml fresh cream

Whipped Egg Yolk

10 egg yolks

METHOD

Mix the oil and the mustard together in a small bowl. Brush the mixture onto the tuna logs. Roll the tuna in the black pepper, leaving the ends without pepper. Heat a dry frying pan until it's very hot and cook the tuna on all sides, searing the fish to about 3 mm in a circle around the edge. You will see how much it is cooked because the circle of ruby flesh will turn brown. Remove from the pan and place on a cool plate.

Place a piece of plastic wrap on a work surface and place the individual pieces of tuna on the plastic. Roll up from the long side and seal the ends by twisting the plastic until the tuna forms a tight, round tube shape. It needs to be very firm. Refrigerate for at least 30 minutes to retain the round shape.

To make the whipped egg yolk, whisk the egg yolks in a mixing bowl and then transfer into a sous vide bag, or use a zip-seal plastic bag. Heat water in a large sauce-pan to 65 °C – use a thermometer to check. Keep the water at roughly this temper-ature by adding blocks of ice if it gets too hot. Place the bag of egg yolks in the hot water and allow to cook for 1–1½ hours. Constantly check the heat of the water, otherwise the egg yolks will 'scramble'.

While the egg yolks are cooking, trim the asparagus ends and cut off the tips, then blanch the tips only for 3 minutes in salted boiling water. Immediately place in ice water to stop the cooking process. Drain and season, and set aside.

Boil the rest of the asparagus until softened and place in a food blender while still warm. Add the cream and blend to a fine purée. Season with salt and pepper and strain through a fine-mesh sieve.

After 1 hour, see if the yolks have thickened. If not, leave to cook for another 30 minutes. Remove from the warm water and place in a bath of ice water to cool down instantly. Transfer the egg yolks from the plastic bag to a mixing bowl. Whisk with an electric mixer or in a stand mixer until the egg yolks are creamy.

Remove the tuna from the fridge and cut into wheels. To serve, spread some as-paragus purée on the plate, then top with the tuna and some fresh asparagus. Use a piping bag and pipe some dots of whipped egg yolk on the plate. Garnish with micro herbs and soya pearls (optional), then serve.

TOMATO FILLED WITH HADDOCK AND A LIGHT APPLE BUTTER, DUSTED WITH POPCORN POWDER

Serves: *28*
Difficulty: *Little effort but easy*
Prep time: *1 hr*
Cooking time: *15 min*

INGREDIENTS

28 small cherry tomatoes

15 ml sea salt

570 g smoked haddock

2 fresh bay leaves

1 L milk

140 ml fresh cream

Juice and zest of 1 lemon

75 g butter, melted

15 ml horseradish sauce

2.5 ml Worcestershire sauce

2.5 ml cayenne pepper

Ground white pepper

Apple Butter

45 ml butter, plus 60 ml cold butter

4 Granny Smith apples, peeled, cored and sliced

5 ml ground cinnamon

50 g sugar

180 ml white wine

125 ml water

15 ml crème fraîche

METHOD

Using a sharp knife, cut a shallow cross through the skin of the tomatoes on the opposite side of the stem. Bring a saucepan of water to a boil and add the salt. Quickly blanch the tomatoes in the boiling water and place immediately in ice water. Remove the skins gently and pat dry on a kitchen cloth. Slice off the bottom of each tomato and carefully scoop out the inside flesh and seeds. Set aside until ready to use.

To make the apple butter, melt the 45 ml butter in a large saucepan over high heat. Add the apples, cinnamon and sugar and stir for about 2 minutes, allowing the apples to sweat without browning. Add the wine and water, cover and cook for 5 minutes until tender. Immediately purée in a blender, adding the 60 ml cold butter as you are blending until it emulsifies. Stir in the crème fraîche and season with salt to taste.

Place the haddock and bay leaves in a saucepan and add the milk. Make sure the fish is covered. Bring to a boil over medium heat, then simmer over low heat for 10 minutes. Drain in a colander and place the fish in a bowl, discarding the skin and any bones. Cool completely. Transfer to a food processor and add the cream, lemon juice and zest. Mix on a medium speed, then add the melted butter, horseradish, Worcestershire sauce and seasoning. If the mixture is too firm, add more cream to get a soft paste.

Place the mixture in a piping bag fitted with a plain nozzle. Pipe the filling into each of the cherry tomatoes, leaving a little room at the top. Fill this space with the apple butter until full. Repeat with all the tomatoes, gently place on wax paper and refrigerate until ready to use.

Serve each filled tomato with a dusting of popcorn powder (see page 131).

4.

MARCHAND DES QUATRE-SAISONS

(Market of the Four Seasons)

The Market of the Four Seasons is a sprawling fruit and vegetable market where I draw daily inspiration. This is where I go when I need to shake up the menu, get ideas for a special event or simply need some fresh air.

For a chef, a visit to the local fresh goods market is a little like window-shopping. You touch, taste, smell and then put in your order for the next morning's delivery. In the process you also get to know the vendors — the delightfully eccentric folk that form the foundation of the market.

At the Market of the Four Seasons, for instance, you'll find the slightly crotchety old lady selling courgette flowers and peaches from her garden from the boot of her car. It will take a few tries, but once you get the hang of subtly bribing her, you'll soon get the best of her produce. And then there are the Mushroom Men who make their way out of the neighbouring Italian forests in the heart of autumn with their fragrant mushrooms and truffles.

It's the singular combination of these fairy-tale characters and their dewy fresh wares that provide the first hints of inspiration for many of the dishes that we serve at JAN.

ROASTED ASPARAGUS AND LEEKS WITH ANCHOVY AND BACON

Serves: *4*
Difficulty: *Easy*
Prep time: *15 min*
Cooking time: *15–20 min*

Retain the delicate flavours by just tying the ingredients together, add a drizzle of good olive oil, a sprinkle of salt and pepper, and place them in the oven for a few minutes until the bacon goes crispy. Serve as a side, one bunch per person.

INGREDIENTS

4 rashers bacon

16 spears green asparagus

8 baby leeks, halved lengthways and washed

4 anchovy fillets

4 sprigs thyme

4 sprigs rosemary

Extra virgin olive oil

1 lemon

Sea salt and ground black pepper

METHOD

Preheat the oven to 180 °C.

Lay the rashers of bacon flat on a working surface and place 4 asparagus spears, 2 leeks and 1 anchovy fillet on top. Place 1 sprig each of thyme and rosemary inside, wrap the bacon around the veg and tie up with kitchen string. Make sure the bunches are nice and tight. Sprinkle with olive oil and squeeze over the juice of the lemon. Season with salt and pepper and place in an ovenproof dish. Roast for 15–20 minutes until the bacon turns crispy.

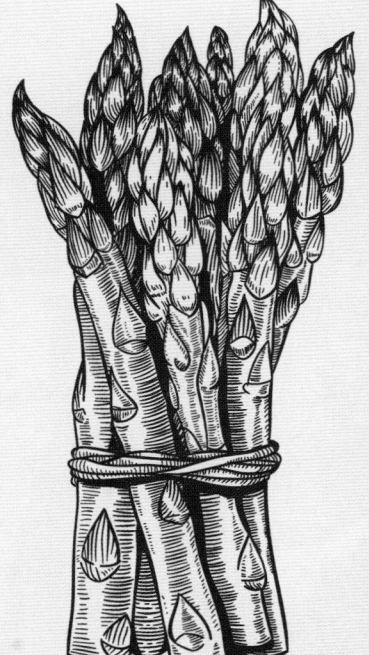

SALT-ROASTED BEETROOT AND GOAT'S CHEESE CRÊPES

Serves: 6
Difficulty: *Easy*
Prep time: *1 hr 45 min*
Cooking time: *1 hr 15 min*

The French invented the curly edged, lacy pancake. Although it sounds like a couture master-piece, it was originally made in Brittany with humble buckwheat or wheat flour and called crêpes de Sarrasin or galettes. It is more basic to the region's gastronomy than bread. Crêper-ies, which dot almost every street in France, serve extensive all-crêpe menus offering fillings ranging from a sprinkling of sugar or a bit of jam to layers of ham, vegetables and cheese. Crêpes are eaten at any time of the day, as a snack or a full meal.

INGREDIENTS

1 kg kosher salt

4 medium beetroots, trimmed

160 g goat's cheese

60 ml crème fraîche

30 ml extra virgin olive oil,
   plus extra

15 ml red wine vinegar

5 ml minced shallot

Sea salt and ground black pepper

1 x Savoury buckwheat crêpe recipe
   (see below)

60 g baby rocket

Juice of ½ lemon

40 g pine nuts, toasted

Savoury Buckwheat Crêpes

3 large organic eggs

60 ml melted butter

375 ml water

30 g white buckwheat flour

120 g whole-buckwheat flour

Salt and ground black pepper

METHOD

Preheat the oven to 180 °C.

Put a layer of half the salt in the bottom of a small baking dish. Place the beetroots on top of the salt. Cover the beetroots with the remaining salt and bake until fork tender, about 1 hour 15 minutes. Remove the beetroots from the salt and leave to cool to room temperature.

To make the dressing, purée the goat's cheese, crème fraîche, olive oil, vinegar and shallot in a food processor until smooth. Season with salt and pepper. Refrigerate until ready to use.

For the crêpes, whisk the eggs, melted butter and water together in a large mixing bowl. Sift together the flours, salt and pepper to taste, then stir into the egg mixture. Cover with plastic wrap and refrigerate overnight.

Add a few drops of oil to a warm pan, smearing it with a piece of paper towel until evenly spread. Add the batter and spread evenly by tilting the pan in all directions. Cook the crêpe over medium to high heat for about 1 minute, or until light brown. Turn over the crêpe by throwing (if you are daring) it or by using a spatula or your fingertips. Cook for 1 minute more. Place on a plate and keep warm while cooking the rest of the batter.

Peel the beets (the skins will slip right off) and cut into small dice. Divide the beets between the buckwheat pancakes. Spoon some of the goat's cheese dressing on top. Drizzle the rocket with fresh lemon juice and olive oil, season with salt and toss. Add the rocket to the pancakes and drizzle again with the goat's cheese dressing. Sprinkle with the toasted pine nuts.

GOLDEN SHALLOT
AND ORANGE CUSTARD

Serves: *4*
Difficulty: *Easy*
Prep time: *40 min*
Cooking time: *1 hr 30 min*

INGREDIENTS

4 shallots, peeled
15 ml unsalted buter
Sea salt and white pepper
5 ml granulated sugar
Freshly grated nutmeg
Zest of 1 orange
2 large eggs
375 ml double cream

Break away from the idea that a custard has to be sweet. Nothing comes close to caramelised shallot — hidden at the bottom of each ramekin — the sweetness and the umami, finished off with a touch of zesty orange. This dish is ideal to make ahead and perfect for vegetarian guests.

METHOD

Preheat the oven to 275 °C.

Using a sharp paring knife, very thinly slice the shallots lengthways, but leave the slices attached at the root end. Use your palm to gently fan out the slices. In a medium-sized pan, melt the butter and add the shallots. Season with salt and white pepper. Sprinkle the sugar and a pinch of nutmeg on top and cook for about 10 minutes until nicely browned. Add the orange zest and cook for another 5 minutes. Set aside to cool slightly.

Fan out the shallots in the centre of four ramekins. In a mixing bowl, beat the eggs with the cream, 2.5 ml salt and white pepper to taste. Add a pinch of nutmeg and pour the mixture into the ramekins. Cover the ramekins with plastic wrap and set in a glass or ceramic dish filled with hot water to reach halfway up the sides of the ramekins. Place the baking dish in the centre of the oven and bake for about 40 minutes, or until a toothpick is inserted and comes out clean. Remove the baking dish from the oven and let the ramekins stand in the water for 5 minutes. Remove the ramekins from the water bath and leave to cool. Serve warm or at room temperature with Shallot Confit (see page 248) and garnished with Caramelised Sunflower Seeds (see page 82, optional).

TOMATO AND CRAB SALAD WITH BASIL PESTO

Serves: *Serves 4*
Difficulty: *Easy*
Prep time: *20 min + 2 hr chilling*
Cooking time: *0 min*

INGREDIENTS

Mixture of fresh tomatoes, washed
*   and quartered*
100 g buffallo mozzarella cheese

Crab Salad
45 ml crème fraîche
15 ml wholegrain mustard
Juice of ½ lime
250 g cooked crab meat (canned,
*   fresh or thawed)*
10 ml minced chives
5 ml green Tabasco sauce
Olive oil
Sea salt and ground black pepper

Basil Pesto
1 clove garlic, peeled
Sea salt
Large bunch basil, leaves picked
*   and washed*
60 g pine nuts
45 ml extra virgin olive oil
60 g Parmesan cheese, grated
Ground black pepper

METHOD

Mix all the ingredients for the crab salad in a large mixing bowl and stir well. Season to taste and refrigerate for at least 2 hours.

To make the basil pesto, bash the garlic in a pestle and mortar with a pinch of salt. Add the basil leaves and pine nuts and crush to a coarse paste. Add the olive oil and stir in the Parmesan, adding a little water if you would like it runnier. Continue until smooth. Season with salt and pepper and refrigerate until ready to use.

To assemble the salad, use a pastry brush to paint a thick line of basil pesto across the centre of each plate. Use a small mould of your choice and create two discs of the crab salad. Mix the tomatoes in a bowl and sprinkle with olive oil, vinegar, salt and pepper, and toss until well covered. Arrange the tomatoes on the basil pesto between the crab salad and top with pieces of buffalo mozzarella. Garnish with fresh herbs.

GLAZED ENDIVE, SPELT AND CARAMELISED SUNFLOWER SEED SALAD

Serves: *4*
Difficulty: *Easy*
Prep time: *15 min*
Cooking time: *1 hr 20 min*

The endive — cousin to chicory — is an under-appreciated bitter-leafed vegetable. It caramelises really well if grilled and then drizzled with honey. A bowl of this fresh salad is a winner alongside a simple steak, and can even be enjoyed as a dish on its own.

INGREDIENTS

3 large endives, washed and halved

125 ml water

5 ml granulated sugar

2.5 ml white wine vinegar

50 ml honey

100 g spelt or barley, rinsed

250 ml Chicken Stock (see
  page 249)

2 cloves garlic

150 g peas, fresh or frozen

60 ml olive oil

4 medium-sized lemons, juiced,
  skin reserved

20 g fresh parsley, roughly chopped

Sea salt and ground black pepper

2 gem lettuces, cut into wedges or
  leaves picked

Caramelised Sunflower Seeds

50 g sunflower seeds

10 ml Chinese five spice

30 ml granulated sugar

Pinch fine sea salt

METHOD

Cut off most of the stalks of the endives and remove several of the leaves. Trim the ends until neat.

Combine the endives, water, sugar, vinegar and honey in a large frying pan over medium heat and bring to a simmer. Make sure the endives are in a single layer in the pan and braise for about 10 minutes, turning occasionally. When pierced with a knife the stalks should be soft. Increase the heat and cook until almost all the liquid has evaporated and the endives are turning golden brown. Caramelise for 5–10 minutes, then remove from the heat and set aside.

Place the spelt or barley in a medium-sized saucepan and cover with the vegetable or chicken stock. Add the garlic and cook over medium heat until all the liquid has evaporated and the spelt is soft. This will take 45–60 minutes. Remove the garlic and strain the spelt. Flatten out on a baking tray and cool in the fridge.

Blanch the peas in boiling water and immediately place in ice water to cool down.

Mix the olive oil and lemon juice with the parsley. Season with salt and pepper.

To caramelise the sunflower seeds, toast the seeds in a nonstick medium-sized pan for about 3 minutes over medium heat. Stir in the five spice and sugar, stirring constantly until the sugar has melted and all the seeds are coated with a thick layer of caramel. Sprinkle with salt and turn out onto wax paper. Allow to cool.

Gently mix the endives, peas, gem lettuce and spelt on a plate and toss with the olive oil and lemon juice dressing. Grate some of the skin from a lemon into the salad and toss. Sprinkle with caramelised sunflower seeds and serve.

VEGETABLE BOUILLON WITH FRESH HERB RAVIOLI

Serves: *4*
Difficulty: *Easy*
Prep time: *3 hr*
Cooking time: *2 hr 30 min*

Bouillon is a fancy word for a broth. It comes from the word bouillir, *meaning to boil. This is a spring favourite and although we serve it in a very small portion between courses, it can be a meal on its own. It is ideal for the seasonal change or just to empty your pantry. Happy boiling!*

INGREDIENTS

4 stalks celery, cleaned and
cut into chunks

2 carrots, peeled and sliced
lengthways

4 baby artichokes, trimmed
(optional)

2 shallots, peeled and studded
with 3 cloves

1 leek, sliced and washed

1 bouquet garni (including thyme
and bay leaf)

5 ml whole black peppercorns

500 ml Chicken Stock (see
page 249)

1 batch Pasta Dough (see page 249)

1 bunch basil leaves

4 sprigs fresh tarragon

1 bunch fresh flat-leaf parsley

150 g Japanese mushrooms or
sliced mushrooms of your choice

Sea salt and ground black pepper

5 ml walnut oil

METHOD

In a large saucepan, mix the celery, carrots, artichokes, shallots, leek, bouquet garni and peppercorns with the stock and simmer on low to medium heat for about 2½ hours, or until the vegetables are soft.

Roll out the pasta dough until 3 mm thick. Cut out 12 squares measuring 5 cm. Place a few leaves of each herb (basil, tarragon, flat-leaf parsley) in the centre of each pasta square and brush the corners with cold water. Fold the one corner over to meet the other and press the sides to close. Cover with a damp cloth and set aside until ready to use.

When the bouillon is nearly ready, add any leftover fresh herbs and the mushrooms to the saucepan, and season with salt and pepper. Cover with the lid and switch off the heat.

Bring a medium-sized saucepan of salted water to a boil. Place the ravioli in the water to cook for 2–5 minutes until *al dente*. Use a slotted spoon to remove the ravioli and drain on paper towel.

Serve the bouillon in a bowl and place the ravioli (three per portion) between the vegetables. Drizzle with a few drops of walnut oil. Serve with fresh bread to soak up all the goodness.

ROASTED BUTTERNUT AND ALMOND QUICHE

Serves: *4–6*
Difficulty: *Easy*
Prep time: *1 hr 45 min*
Cooking time: *45 min*

Friday lunch at JAN calls for something quick, seasonal and full of flavour. We also serve a square of this delicious quiche with our main courses during the autumn and winter months. The beauty of this quiche is not only its texture, but also the nuttiness that complements the butternut so well. Serve with a dollop of crème fraîche and a sprinkling of chopped chives.

INGREDIENTS

Crust
100 g all-purpose flour
50 g almond flour
75 g salted butter, at room temperature
1 egg yolk
Fine sea salt

Filling
500 g butternut, seeded and diced
Olive oil for drizzling
Fine sea salt and ground black pepper
3 eggs
20 ml unsalted butter, melted
100 g almond flour
100 g Comté or strong Cheddar cheese, grated
Pinch nutmeg
Pinch ground allspice
Pinch ground cumin
50 g flaked almonds

METHOD

Preheat the oven to 180 °C.

For the crust, use your fingers to combine the flours and the butter in a large mixing bowl. Add the egg yolk and salt and mix until a dough forms. If necessary, add ice water if the dough is not soft enough. Cover with plastic wrap and refrigerate for 1 hour.

To make the filling, place the butternut cubes on a baking tray, drizzle with some olive oil and season with salt and pepper. Roast in the preheated oven for 15 minutes, or until the butternut is soft. Transfer the butternut to a food processor and blend until it forms a smooth purée. Spoon the mixture into a mixing bowl and add the eggs, melted butter, almond flour, cheese and spices. Mix well with a wooden spoon until well combined. Season with salt and pepper.

Spray a quiche pan or cake tin with nonstick spray. Roll out the dough on a lightly floured surface and gently lift the pastry by placing the edge on the rolling pin and carefully lifting it. Place in the quiche pan and press lightly with your fingers until even. Cut a piece of baking paper and place it inside the pan. Fill with rice or baking beans and bake in the preheated oven for 10–15 minutes until the crust is golden. Remove and leave to cool.

Fill the pastry shell with the butternut egg mixture and bake at 180 °C for about 45 minutes. Sprinkle with the flaked almonds a few minutes before the end of the cooking time. Serve warm.

Tip: The following butternut/pumpkin spice mix makes a lovely gift, packaged in a pretty jar – 80 ml ground cinnamon, 15 ml ground ginger, 15 ml ground nutmeg or mace, 7.5 ml ground cloves, 7.5 ml ground allspice

5.

BOUCHERIE

[buʃRi] (commerce) butcher's, butchers shop,
(=métier) butchery, (fig.) slaughter

When you run a busy restaurant it is vital to cultivate a good
relationship with your butcher. You need to know where your meat
comes from and that you can call on them at any time of day.

In France it takes some doing. Our butcher is in Cannes, a few
minutes from Nice, and it took years to get to the point where
I can now comfortably request the magret de canard, côte de
boeuf and rich veal bones to simmer down to our trademark silky
sauces. What started as halted, awkward conversations in my
broken French has now, thankfully, blossomed into a mutually
beneficial relationship where I teach them English and they
guide me along the linguistic intricacies of French.

CHICKEN LIVER
AND PARMESAN MOUSSE

Serves: *4*

Difficulty: *Easy*

Prep time: *2 hr + chilling time*
  + overnight for soaking livers

Cooking time: *15 min*

INGREDIENTS

Chicken Liver Mousse

800 g fresh chicken livers

800 ml milk

300 g butter

2 fresh bay leaves

Bunch fresh thyme, leaves picked

5 shallots, finely diced

4 cloves garlic, chopped

Extra virgin olive oil

250 ml sherry

5 ml ground white pepper

2.5 ml grated nutmeg

2.5 ml ground cinnamon

2.5 ml ground allspice

250 ml brandy

120 ml fresh cream

Parmesan Mousse

310 ml fresh cream

14 g or 2 sheets of gelatine

50 g Parmesan cheese, grated

Ground black pepper

4 spring onions

2 radishes, halved and scooped out

This recipe was inspired by the flavours from my mother's kitchen and her famous chicken liver parfait. Summer doesn't get much more summery than the aroma of cherries poaching in spiced red wine.

METHOD

Soak the livers overnight in the milk, then drain. Trim off any connective tissue and dry on paper towel. Dice half of the butter and leave it at room temperature. Melt the rest of the butter in a small saucepan with the bay leaves and thyme. Set aside to infuse. In a medium-sized saucepan, sweat the shallots and garlic with a dash of the olive oil until softened. Add the sherry and reduce to just below half.

Mix all the spices together. Lightly oil the livers and sear them in a large saucepan over high heat in three batches, seasoning well with salt as you go. Gradually add the diced butter and spices and then finish off with a dash of brandy to deglaze the pan. Strain the leftover brandy in a separate container before wiping out the pan and repeating with each batch.

Remove the bay leaves and thyme from the melted butter by straining it through a fine-mesh sieve. Place the livers, reserved brandy and the shallot mixture in a blender, in two batches, and purée, adding the cream and the melted butter as you go. Mix the batches together, check for seasoning and pass though a fine-mesh sieve. Place the mousse into a piping bag fitted with a plain nozzle and refrigerate until needed.

For the Parmesan mousse, bring the cream to a boil in a saucepan. Remove from the heat as soon as it has reached a boil. Soften the gelatine in cold water, then add to the cream. Add the grated Parmesan and pepper and whisk well. Refrigerate for 2 hours. Transfer the mousse to a pastry bag fitted with a small tip.

To assemble the plate, cut the spring onions in half lengthways and roast on a very hot griddle pan with a dash of olive oil. Pipe the liver and Parmesan mousses into the hollows in the radishes and here and there on the plate. Garnish with poached cherries*, Red Wine Gel (see page 253), ginger biscuit crumbs and seasonal berries.

* Poached cherries: Bring 100 ml port and 50 g granulated sugar to a simmer and add 8 cherries (stems intact). Poach until the liquid has been absorbed but the cherries are still firm. Refrigerate until needed.

PORK TERRINE WITH MARINATED VEGETABLES

Serves: *10*

Difficulty: *Medium*

Prep time: *40 min +*
3–4 hr marinating

Cooking time: *1 hr 30 min*

INGREDIENTS

Pork Terrine

15 ml olive oil, plus extra

200 g shallots, finely chopped

550 g pork shoulder, minced by
your butcher or cut into small
pieces and pulsed in a blender

200 g streaky bacon, chopped

350 g sausage meat

45 ml port

Small bunch fresh thyme, chopped

Small bunch fresh parsley, chopped

2.5 ml ground allspice

1 ml ground cloves

5 ml fine sea salt

2.5 ml ground black pepper

3 cloves garlic

15 dried juniper berries, crushed

130 g pistachios, roughly chopped

Marinated Vegetables

250 ml white wine vinegar

250 ml water

30 ml granulated sugar

30 ml fine sea salt

Baby vegetables of your choice

Considered to be slightly intimidating in the kitchen, the terrine is a 'once you know how' kind of dish that you will always go back to for entertaining larger groups. It's great to make ahead of time and fabulous for sharing at a large table of food lovers.

METHOD

To make the terrine, heat the oil in a large pan and soften the shallots for about 10 minutes. Remove from the heat and allow to cool. Mix all the other terrine ingredients in a large mixing bowl and fry a small portion in a pan, then taste and adjust the seasoning.

Preheat the oven to 160 °C. Line a terrine dish or loaf tin with greaseproof paper and fill with the terrine mixture, making sure it gets into the corners. Cover with oiled foil, place in a deep roasting pan and fill with boiling water to come halfway up the sides of the terrine dish. Bake for 1 hour to 1 hour 15 minutes. Remove the foil, drain the excess juices and return to the oven for another 15 minutes. The terrine should be firm.

Remove from the roasting pan and cool for 15 minutes. Discard any more liquid and then cover with plastic wrap, place a piece of cardboard on top (cut to fit inside the tin), then rest four cans or other weights on top. Leave to cool completely before turning out.

To make the marinated vegetables, bring the vinegar, water, sugar and salt to a boil in a small saucepan until the sugar has dissolved. Place the vegetables in the liquid while it is still hot. The vegetables will rise to the top so use a plastic lid or a smaller cover to immerse the vegetables in the marinating liquid. Marinate for 3–4 hours.

To serve, place a slice of terrine on each plate and arrange the marinated vegetables neatly on top.

SLOW-BRAISED PORK BELLY WITH BEETROOTS

Serves: *4*

Difficulty: *Medium*

Prep time: *30 min +*
   24 hr marinating

Cooking time: *4–5 hr*

INGREDIENTS

500 g lean, boneless pork belly,
   skin on

Zest and juice of 1 lime

200 g fresh pineapple, diced

3 lemon leaves, crushed

2 cinnamon sticks

4 star anise

5 whole cloves

5 cm piece fresh ginger, peeled and
   finely chopped

2 cloves garlic, crushed

Sea salt and ground black pepper

Extra virgin olive oil

1 onion, roughly chopped

2 leeks, washed and chopped

2 carrots, peeled and chopped

500 ml Chicken Stock (see
   page 249) or Brown Beef Stock
   (see page 251)

500 g baby beetroots, scrubbed,
   with stems intact

50 g butter

50 ml honey

60 ml balsamic vinegar

Baby beetroot leaves

The belly is the pig's greatest culinary gift; just make sure you source from a butcher you have a good relationship with. The crispy fat and the earthiness of the beetroots make this dish a real crowd-pleaser.

METHOD

Score the pork to allow the fat to render out and crisp up when grilling. Place it skin-side down in a bowl or container. Cover with half the lime juice and zest, the diced pineapple with its juice, lemon leaves, cinnamon sticks, star anise, cloves, ginger and garlic. Season lightly with salt and pepper and leave for 24 hours in the fridge for the flavours to infuse.

The following day, heat a little olive oil in a heavy-based saucepan or roasting pan and caramelise the onion, leeks and carrots. Add the pork, skin-side down, and pour in the stock until the meat is just covered. Bring to a boil and cover with a lid or foil to retain the moisture. Slow-cook for 4–5 hours. Alternatively, place the dish in the oven at 160 °C and bake for 3 hours. Once cooked, a knife should easily push through the flesh and the fat should be gelatinous.

Remove the pork from the liquid (reserve the liquid and strain it) and gently place a weight on top to press the whole belly flat. (A heap of plates or a kitchen weight is ideal.) Refrigerate until fully cooled. Remove any excess jelly or cooking juices and cut the belly into small pieces. Lightly oil a griddle pan and place over moderate heat. Add the pork, skin-side down, and cook until coloured. Then place the pork belly, skin-side up, under a moderately hot grill. Reduce the strained liquid in a saucepan until it has the consistency of a jus. Strain again through muslin cloth or a fine-mesh sieve. Set aside.

For the beetroots, preheat the oven to 190 °C. Boil the baby beetroots for 20 minutes, drain and leave until they are cool enough to handle. Peel them carefully without breaking off the stems. The skin should come off easily. Halve the beetroots and toss with butter, honey and seasoning. Bake for 10 minutes and then sprinkle with balsamic vinegar and bake for a further 10–15 minutes. Cover with foil and set aside.

To assemble, arrange the squares of pork belly and beetroot randomly on each plate, drizzle with the reduced jus and scatter over fresh baby beetroot leaves. Serve with very thinly sliced beetroot tossed in olive, vinegar and seasoning, if desired.

VEAL CHEEKS COOKED IN RED WINE WITH FOIE GRAS

Serves: *10*

Difficulty: *Medium*

Prep time: *30 min + overnight for marinating*

Cooking time: *2–3 hr*

INGREDIENTS

4 cloves garlic

1.25 L light red wine

1 onion, roughly chopped

1 leek, trimmed, rinsed and roughly chopped

1 medium-sized carrot, peeled and roughly chopped

3 sprigs fresh rosemary

4 sprigs fresh thyme

30 ml blackberry jam

2 cinnamon sticks

12 veal cheeks

10 ml granulated sugar

30 ml extra virgin olive oil

Freshly ground sea salt and black pepper

750 ml Brown Beef Stock (see page 251)

1 lobe foie gras, frozen

A little bit exotic and on the richer side, but a winter favourite. The foie gras adds a touch of luxury, but the dish is just as good without it.

METHOD

Crush the garlic and combine it with the red wine, onion, leek, carrot, rosemary, thyme, blackberry jam and cinnamon. Place the veal cheeks in this marinade, cover and refrigerate overnight.

The following day, preheat the oven to 200 °C. Remove the cheeks from the marinade, pat dry and set aside. Strain the marinade through a fine-mesh sieve, reserving the strained vegetables.

Place the strained marinade and the sugar in a saucepan and simmer over medium heat until the marinade has reduced by half. Skim off any foam that appears on the surface. Spread the reserved vegetables in a layer across the bottom of a roasting pan. Roast the vegetables in the oven for 15–20 minutes until browned and caramelised.

Heat the olive oil in a large sauté pan over medium heat. Season the veal cheeks with salt and pepper and place them in the pan, searing on each side for about 2 minutes. Transfer to a plate and set aside.

Once the vegetables in the roasting pan have caramelised, reduce the oven temperature to 150 °C. Lay the browned cheeks on top of the vegetables — do not overlap — and pour the reduced marinade over the top. Add enough stock to cover the cheeks. Cover the roasting pan with foil, pressing down until the foil touches the veal cheeks. Bake for 2–3 hours until the meat is tender and falls apart easily.

Remove the roasting pan from the oven and, using a slotted spoon, carefully transfer the veal cheeks to a plate and keep warm. Strain the sauce through a fine-mesh sieve into a bowl and discard the remaining solids. Skim off the fat with a ladle.

Use a plane grater and grate the frozen foie gras into a small container. Immediately return to the freezer to keep frozen until needed.

Serve the veal cheeks with roasted turnips, Parsnip Purée (see page 253) and the grated foie gras, and drizzle with the jus.

MAGRET DE CANARD WITH TONKA JUS

Serves: *4*

Difficulty: *Medium*

Prep time: *30 min + 8 hr marinating (or overnight)*

Cooking time: *10–15 min*

INGREDIENTS

2 large magret de canard (fatty duck breasts)

2.5 ml sea salt

Ground black pepper

45 ml honey

Fresh thyme

125 ml orange juice

750 ml Brown Beef Stock (see page 251)

3 tonka beans (or vanilla or coffee beans)

250 ml port

150 ml blackberry jam

The French love duck, and to get a good piece of Magret de canard that is cooked to perfection might leave you with a love for this sweet, rich meat forever. Seasonal fruit such as apples, oranges or cherries make for a perfect combination.

METHOD

Use a sharp knife to score the fat on top of the duck breasts into small diamond shapes. Cut halfway through the fat but not all the way through to the meat. Rub the breasts on both sides with salt and pepper and smear with the honey and thyme. Place in a sous vide or zip seal plastic bag and pour in the orange juice. Squeeze out as much air as possible, seal the bag and refrigerate for up to 8 hours.

Just before you are ready to cook the breasts, preheat the oven to 200 °C. Remove the breasts from the marinade, discarding any sprigs of thyme and dry with paper towels. Set the marinade aside. Place the duck fat-side down onto a cold iron skillet or any other heavy-based ovenproof skillet. Turn the heat up to medium and let the fat render from the duck breasts for about 5 minutes. Turn the heat up and cook for another 3–4 minutes until most of the fat has turned into oil. Drain the fat and reserve for another use. Place the duck breasts in the skillet in the oven for 5 minutes until medium-rare. Remove from the oven and allow to rest on a cutting board for 5 minutes.

In a small saucepan, mix the marinade, beef stock, tonka beans, port and black-berry jam and reduce to a syrupy consistency. Strain through a fine-mesh sieve.

Slice the duck breasts thinly and serve with the tonka jus.

ROAST BEEF FILLET WITH CHESTNUTS AND MUSHROOMS

Serves: *4*
Difficulty: *Easy*
Prep time: *25 min*
Cooking time: *45 min*

The small town of Apricale in Italy, which lies 40 minutes south of Nice, is where I spend my weekends eating and drinking among the Italians. Typically, Italians serve anything from six to seven courses of pastas, meats, more pastas and more meats. Simplicity is the key to these earthy flavours.

INGREDIENTS

1 kg beef fillet
45 ml butter
15 ml olive oil
Sea salt and ground black pepper
1 stalk celery, chopped
1 carrot, peeled and chopped
1 leek, washed and chopped
1 onion, chopped
1 sprig fresh rosemary, chopped
75 ml dry white wine
800 g dried (soaked for 6 hr in
  water) or canned whole chestnuts
500 g white mushrooms
45 ml heavy cream

METHOD

Preheat the oven to 200 °C. Tie the meat neatly with kitchen string to form a lobe. Heat 30 ml of the butter and the oil in a large roasting pan and add the meat, turning frequently to sear and brown it all over. Season with salt and pepper and add the celery, carrot, leek, onion and rosemary. Cook and stir occasionally for another 10 minutes. Add the wine and cook for a few minutes until it has evaporated. Cover with a lid or foil and place in the oven for 30–40 minutes, depending on how you want the meat done. After 30 minutes the beef will be rare and after 40 minutes it will be medium.

If you are using dried chestnuts, boil them in water until tender (up to 20 minutes). Drain and set aside.

Remove the fillet from the oven and let it stand for about 10 minutes, then remove the string and carve. In the roasting pan used for the fillet, cook the mushrooms and chestnuts in the remaining 15 ml butter over low heat until lightly browned. Stir in the cream and cook until slightly thickened. Pour the sauce over the fillet and serve immediately.

ROAST LAMB WITH STUFFED PUMPKIN FLOWERS

INGREDIENTS

1.2 kg shoulder of lamb, deboned

12 pumpkin or courgette flowers

Vegetable oil for deep-frying

Lamb Filling

4 sprigs fresh flat-leaf parsley

5 sprigs fresh thyme

5 springs fresh rosemary

4 cloves garlic

Zest of 2 lemons

Extra virgin olive oil

Crust

1 clove garlic, finely chopped

60 g ground almonds

5 ml lemon juice

50 g green olives, pitted

20 ml extra virgin olive oil

Sea salt and ground black pepper

Flower Filling

250 g ricotta cheese

2 anchovies

Zest of 1 lemon

30 ml lemon juice

Bunch fresh parsley and mint

Flower Batter

1 egg

± 250 ml ice-cold sparkling water

160 g all-purpose flour

Pinch fine salt

Serves: *4*

Difficulty: *Easy*

Prep time: *25 min*

Cooking time: *45 min*

This leg of lamb is tender and juicy, with a flavourful herbed crust. We plate it in smaller portions at JAN, but it's perfect served on a large platter with roast spring vegetables for a gathering of family or friends.

METHOD

Preheat the oven to 200 °C. Remove the lamb from the fridge and allow to reach room temperature. Rinse the herbs and place in a blender with the garlic, lemon zest and olive oil. Blend until mixed (it does not have to be very fine).

Prepare the crust. Mix the garlic, ground almonds, lemon juice, green olives and 30 ml of the herb filling. Add olive oil and season with salt and pepper.

Butterfly the leg of lamb if not already done by your butcher, and spread the herb gremolata thickly over the meat. Roll up and tie up with kitchen string. Place in a roasting pan and cover with the crust mixture. Roast for 45 minutes, or until the lamb is cooked but still pink inside. Set aside to rest.

While the lamb is roasting, mix the ricotta, anchovies, lemon zest and juice, parsley and mint. Season with salt and pepper. Carefully stuff the pumpkin flowers with the mixture and close the ends gently. Mix all the flower batter ingredients with a fork until combined. Add the sparkling water a little at a time so that the batter is of a slightly thinner consistency than that of a pancake batter.

Warm a medium-sized pot with vegetable oil for deep-frying. Dip the stuffed flowers carefully into the batter and then place in the hot oil. Cook just until the crust turns crisp. Remove and place on paper towel to absorb the excess oil.

Serve warm with slices of lamb.

LAMB SHANK WITH PARMESAN CRUMB CRUST

Serves: 6
Difficulty: *Little effort but easy*
Prep time: *24 hr*
Cooking time: *2 hr 30 min*

Soaking the lamb shanks in brine overnight adds so much more depth to the meat. And if you braise the shanks a day ahead, you will notice how the flavour improves even more overnight. Although this dish may take some time, the moment that meat falls off the bone you will thank yourself a hundred times over!

INGREDIENTS

4 L water

100 g granulated sugar

170 g sea salt

6 lamb shanks

Sea salt and ground black pepper

Flour for coating the shanks

Extra virgin olive oil

240 g canned tomatoes, crushed

2 carrots, chopped

3 stalks celery, chopped

1 large onion, chopped

1 bulb fresh fennel, chopped

4 cloves garlic, chopped

5 ml fennel seeds

250 ml red wine

250 ml water

*10 sprigs each fresh flat-leaf
   parsley and rosemary, chopped*

Crust

*60 g unsalted butter, at room
   temperature*

60 ml Panko breadcrumbs

20 g Parmesan cheese, grated

2 cloves garlic, minced

Ground black pepper

METHOD

Place the water, sugar and salt into a large container. Carefully add the lamb shanks and soak for 24 hours in the fridge.

The following day, preheat the oven to 180 °C. Remove the shanks from the brine mixture and dry with paper towels. Season well and coat with the flour before browning them in olive oil on medium-high heat until golden brown – about 4 minutes each side.

Place the shanks in a large roasting pan with the crushed tomatoes. In the same pan that the shanks were seared in, sauté the carrots, celery, onion, fennel, garlic and fennel seeds. Add the red wine and 250 ml water to deglaze the pan and then transfer the mixture to the roasting pan. Add the parsley and rosemary, cover with foil and roast for 2 hours, or until very tender. After about 1 hour, turn the shanks and cover for the remaining time, ensuring the shanks are covered in liquid.

Make the crust by mixing all the ingredients together and mashing it up to form a dough-like mixture. This is also better if made in advance – it usually takes 2–3 hours to develop great flavour. Place the 'dough' in plastic wrap and flatten it (this will make it easier to work with). Remove the shanks from the roasting pan and press pieces of the dough onto the lamb shanks. Place the shanks in a clean ovenproof dish and roast at 200 °C for about 30 minutes until browned.

6.
POISSONNERIE

[pwa.sɔn.ʁi] fishmonger, fish market

In the south of France, fish and seafood is such an important part of the local cuisine that it is absolutely imperative to have a reliable fishmonger.

At JAN, our fish is delivered at the crack of dawn by a shy young boy whose initial grasp of the English language only extended far enough to include the most important term in the fishmonger's repertoire: 'very fresh'. He finds our culturally eclectic kitchen quite intriguing, and we happily teach him a few shreds of English when he brings around his silvery wares, leaving behind the distinctive smell of fresh seawater.

STUFFED SARDINES WITH LEMON AND ROASTED ONIONS

Serves: *4*
Difficulty: *Easy*
Prep time: *1 hr*
Cooking time: *20 min*

These small fish are inexpensive, tasty and nutritious which explains why they are so popular in the Mediterranean diet. They must be scaled and cleaned before cooking and, if preferred, you can also cut off the heads and remove the bones.

INGREDIENTS

½ bunch fresh flat-leaf parsley
1 clove garlic
3 eggs
45 ml breadcrumbs
30 ml freshly grated Parmesan
    cheese
Sea salt and ground black pepper
Zest and juice of 1 lemon
500 g fresh sardines, scaled,
    cleaned and deboned
All-purpose flour for dusting
75 ml extra virgin olive oil
8 spring onions

METHOD

Chop the parsley and garlic together, place in a bowl and add the eggs. Beat well. Add the breadcrumbs and Parmesan and season with salt and pepper. Add the lemon zest and mix again.

Spread the mixture over the opened sardines, fold them back together and dust lightly with the flour. Shake off any excess. Heat the oil in a large frying pan and add the sardines – cook for 5–6 minutes, turning once. Add some lemon juice, remove with a slotted spatula and drain on paper towel. Season with salt and pepper.

Cut the spring onions in half lengthways and toss them with little olive oil. Grill them in a hot pan over high heat. Sprinkle with salt and pepper. Serve with the sardines and slices of lemon.

SEARED SCALLOPS WITH LEMONY SALSA VERDE

Serves: *4*
Difficulty: *Easy*
Prep time: *15 min*
Cooking time: *3 min*

INGREDIENTS

50 g butter

30 ml extra virgin olive oil

12 fresh scallops or shellfish of your choice

Salsa Verde

½ lemon with peel, seeded and chopped

1 small shallot, finely chopped

1 clove garlic, finely chopped

Sea salt and ground black pepper

250 ml extra virgin olive oil

180 ml chopped fresh parsley

125 ml finely chopped fresh coriander

60 ml chopped chives

The simplicity of a pan-kissed scallop and lemon, garlic and shallots. A bright, fresh intermediate course.

METHOD

Make the salsa verde first. Combine the lemon, shallot, garlic and seasoning in a bowl. Allow to stand for 5 minutes, then stir in the 250 ml olive oil, parsley, coriander and chives. Adjust seasoning and add lemon juice if needed.

Heat the butter and 30 ml olive oil in a large nonstick pan over medium heat. Season the scallops and place in the warm pan to sear on both sides, about 1½ minutes per side. Serve while still hot with the salsa verde.

BOURRIDE

Serves: 6
Difficulty: *Medium*
Prep time: *30 min*
Cooking time: *30 min*

INGREDIENTS

Aïoli

½ small clove garlic, crushed

1 large egg yolk

Sea salt and ground black pepper

Lemon juice to taste

Zest of 1 lemon

5 ml Dijon mustard

300 ml olive oil

300 ml grapeseed oil

Bourride

60 ml extra virgin olive oil

5 ml fennel seeds

5 ml anise seeds

2.5 ml cayenne pepper

2 cloves garlic, crushed

2 leeks, white part only, chopped

2 onions, roughly chopped

3 ripe tomatoes, chopped

1 dried bay leaf

1 L Fish Stock (see page 250)

500 ml dry white wine

6 large prawns, peeled and deveined

1 kg firm white fish, cod, hake or
    similar, bones removed

6 baby fennel, trimmed

2.5 ml saffron threads

There are a few dishes in France that invite polemic to the table, including cassoulet, French onion soup, salade Niçoise and, of course, bouillabaisse. It can get out of hand sometimes and turn into a discussion more volatile than politics or religion.

Bourride is the cousin of the bouillabaisse, which earned its name from a similar type of dish. In plain language, it's a fish stew. The only differences really are that the bourride includes less of a variety of fish, the fish is usually cut into pieces and the broth is thickened with an aïoli, and it is finished off with saffron and fennel. Bouillabaisse, on the other hand, consists of whole fish, normally seven different species from the Mediterranean…

METHOD

To make the aïoli, whisk the garlic, egg yolk, seasoning, lemon juice, lemon zest and mustard in a mixing bowl and slowly add the oils. Keep whisking until the texture resembles that of a mayonnaise. Alternatively, use a blender. Taste and adjust seasoning.

For the bourride, heat the oil in a large saucepan over medium heat. Add the fennel and anise seeds and cayenne and roast for a few minutes, then add the garlic, leeks, onions, tomatoes and bay leaf. Cook for 15–20 minutes until caramelised. Add the stock and wine, boil and reduce by half. Strain the mixture and return to the saucepan over medium heat. Remove the heads and tails from the prawns but retain the heads. Add the fish, prawns and heads, baby fennel and saffron. Season to taste. Cook for 2–3 minutes until the fish is almost cooked and the prawns turn pink. (The fish will continue cooking in the warm liquid so be careful not to overcook it.)

Use a slotted spoon and divide the fish and prawns between plates. Whisk 125 ml of the broth with 30 ml of the aïoli (store the rest in the refrigerator for up to four days), return to the saucepan and cook until slightly thickened. Ladle over the fish, garnish each plate with a prawn head and serve with toasted baguette on the side.

COFFEE AND VODKA SALMON GRAVLAX WITH EGG YOLK CREAM

Serves: *6*
Difficulty: *Medium*
Prep time: *6 hr*
Cooking time: *0 min*

With the number of Scandinavians, Russians and Italians we host at JAN, this has won a special place in most of their culinary hearts. This dish can be improvised with seasonal vegetables such as asparagus, avocados or artichokes. Let the season predict the final outcome, as we always do at JAN.

INGREDIENTS

1 kg coarse salt
4 Nespresso™ capsules, opened
230 ml vodka
1 salmon fillet, skinned and
  deboned
1 batch Whipped Egg Yolk
  (see page 61)

METHOD

In a large roasting pan, combine the salt, coffee powder from the capsules and the vodka and mix until well combined. Gently place the salmon fillet on top of the salt and cover with the salt lying around the salmon, so the entire fillet is covered. Cover with plastic wrap and refrigerate for 6 hours.

Once ready, wash off the salt mixture and dry the salmon with paper towels. Slice into thin portions and serve with the whipped egg yolk, blanched asparagus and avocado.

SALMON IN
A HERB GARDEN

Serves: 6
Difficulty: *Easy*
Prep time: *30 min*
Cooking time: *5 min*

INGREDIENTS

3 portions salmon fillet

Sea salt and ground black pepper

15 ml extra virgin olive oil

200 ml coconut milk

1 avocado

Juice of 3 limes

15 ml white balsamic vinegar
  (optional)

10 ml fish sauce

5 ml granulated sugar

3 ml green Tabasco sauce

1 bunch each fresh coriander, mint,
  chives and dill

100 ml cream cheese

10 ml wasabi paste

1 Granny Smith apple, sliced with
  a mandoline into very thin
  circles or into thin 'sticks'

1 bulb fresh fennel, sliced very
  thinly with a mandoline

50 g fish eggs or caviar (optional)

The intriguing name describes exactly what it is. A selection of fresh herbs, coconut milk, lime and avocado with a seared piece of salmon, a dash of wasabi cream and fish eggs.

METHOD

Cut the salmon into portions small enough for a starter or larger if doing a main course. Season with salt and pepper. Heat the olive oil in a medium-sized nonstick pan and sear the salmon quickly – 10–15 seconds per side. It must still be pink in the centre. Dry on paper towels and place in a container in the fridge until needed.

In a blender, combine the coconut milk, avocado, lime juice, vinegar, fish sauce, sugar, Tabasco and the herbs. Blend until the mixture is smooth and the herbs are blended in. Season with salt and pepper and adjust flavour. Refrigerate until needed.

In a small bowl, mix the cream cheese and wasabi together and season to taste.

To serve, pour some coconut herb sauce in the centre of each plate and top with a portion of salmon. Arrange freshly picked herbs in and around the salmon. Garnish with the apple and fennel slices and add a dollop of wasabi cream topped with fish eggs.

BAKED TROUT
PROVENÇALE

Serves: *4*
Difficulty: *Easy*
Prep time: *30 min*
Cooking time: *20–30 min*

INGREDIENTS

4 trout, deboned and butterflied
Sea salt and ground black pepper
30 ml extra virgin olive oil
1 medium-sized onion, chopped
3 cloves garlic, minced
300 g fresh tomatoes, chopped or
   240 g canned tomatoes
Pinch granulated sugar (optional)
30 ml chopped fresh basil
12 black olives, pitted
4 sprigs fresh thyme
12 red pepper fillets (the sides of
   the pepper)

Although this Provençal favourite is served during summer when the tomatoes are at their plummest, it is also successful with canned tomatoes.

METHOD

Preheat the oven to 200 °C. Grease a large baking dish big enough to accommodate all the fish in a single layer. If they don't fit into one, use two. Open up the trout and season with salt and pepper.

Heat the olive oil in a large, heavy-based saucepan over medium heat. Add the onion and cook until soft. Add the garlic and cook for 30 seconds, then mix in the tomatoes and sugar. When it starts to boil, turn down the heat to medium-low and simmer for 15 minutes until the sauce is thick and fragrant. Stir in the basil and olives, and season to taste.

Place a spoonful of tomato sauce and a sprig of thyme on one half of each butterflied trout and close up. Lay side by side in the baking dish and spread the remaining sauce over the fish. Place the red pepper fillets randomly among the fish and cover with lightly oiled foil. Bake for 10–15 minutes until the fish pulls apart easily when tested with a fork.

Serve the fish with the sauce, red peppers, shaved butternut that is dressed in olive oil and raspberry vinegar, and slices of grilled potatoes.

COD WITH CORN, CAULIFLOWER AND POPCORN POWDER

Serves: *4–6*
Difficulty: *Easy*
Prep time: *20 min*
Cooking time: *20 min*

Any white fish will work for this recipe. On a recent visit to my parents' farm in Mpumalanga I had to do one evening of 'smart food' and used hake with fresh corn from the harvest. The extras on the plate can be varied with a fresh salad or, if you fancy a similar plate, use carrot purée, ginger gel and popcorn powder.

INGREDIENTS

4–6 cod or hake fillets
Sea salt and ground black pepper
90 ml extra virgin olive oil
45 ml butter
4 corn on the cob, grilled quite
  dark and cut off the cobs
1 head cauliflower, cut into small
  florets and blanched

Popcorn Powder
15 ml sunflower or grapeseed oil
180 g popcorn kernels
15 ml fine sea salt
15 ml sugar
5 ml cayenne pepper (optional)

METHOD

Make the popcorn powder first. Heat the oil in a large saucepan until hot. Add the popcorn kernels and cover with a lid. Keep shaking the saucepan until the popping has come to a stop. Remove from the heat and transfer to a large baking tray. Carefully pick out the kernels that didn't pop and discard them. Season the popcorn with salt, sugar and cayenne pepper and place the mixture in a blender. Use both hands to shake the blender while it is in action so that it blends evenly. The popcorn should resemble a fine powder. Place in an airtight container until ready to use.

Season the fish fillets on both sides. In a large skillet, heat 60 ml of the olive oil and 30 ml of the butter. When the pan is hot, add the fish fillets and cook until golden brown and the fish flakes easily. Depending on the thickness it should take about 3 minutes on each side.

In a separate medium-sized pan, warm the remaining 30 ml oil and 15 ml butter over medium heat. Add the corn, cauliflower and seasoning. Sauté until the corn and cauliflower are soft and warm.

Serve the fish with the corn and cauliflower, Carrot Purée (see page 252) and Ginger Gel (see page 253). Dust each portion with 5 ml popcorn powder.

7.

FROMAGERIE

[fro-ma-gi-rie] (*fromager', fromage', fromage de tête', flagornerie'*)
a cheese factory/location where cheese is produced and sold

A love of cheese is synonymous with a love of France, a country whose citizens are so enamoured with this dairy staple that they have succeeded in identifying more than a thousand different ways to make it. From Abondance to Gruyère, Roquefort and Valençay, each cheese has a unique flavour profile reminiscent of the region that first produced it.

The gentleman who supplies our restaurant has mysterious connections and always succeeds in procuring from deep in the mountains rare cheeses that you wouldn't find on the supermarket shelf. These wonderful finds are still made by hand and you can literally taste the difference in the milk they use as the seasons change — in springtime there are distinctly herbal, flowery notes; in winter a delightful concentrated earthiness. With this kind of cheese at your disposal is it any wonder that the average French citizen (myself included) would not see a day complete without a stop at the fromagerie with a fresh baguette beneath one arm?

CAMEMBERT AND COGNAC-SOAKED BERRY CAKE

Serves: *1 Camembert-sized cake*
Difficulty: *Easy*
Prep time: *2 hr 20 min (incl soaking time)*
Baking time: *15 min*

INGREDIENTS

1 Camembert, cold and firm
320 g dried fruit, such as cranberries, raisins, prunes and goji berries
125 ml cognac or good-quality brandy
125 ml lukewarm water
1 roll (400 g) puff pastry
1 egg, beaten

This easy-to-put-together cake is great for entertaining larger groups, ideal for a cheeseboard or to serve as a snack at apéritif hour.

METHOD

Use a sharp knife to cut the Camembert horizontally into two even layers. Set aside on a tray lined with wax paper.

Combine all the dried fruit in a small saucepan, add the cognac and water and simmer for 15 minutes over low heat. Make sure all the fruit is covered with liquid. If necessary, add another 60 ml water or cognac. Stir to moisten all the fruit. Transfer to a large bowl and cover loosely with plastic wrap. Let the fruit soak for about 2 hours, or until it is moist and plumped up.

Preheat the oven to 200 °C. Cut the pastry into two circles slightly larger than the container of the Camembert. Brush with the egg wash, place on a baking tray and bake for 15 minutes. Place the pastry on a cooling rack and allow to cool slightly before stacking it with the sliced Camembert and layers of soaked fruit in between.

OLIVE AND ROSEMARY STICKS WITH WHIPPED MISO BUTTER

GIFT IDEA

Makes: *30*
Difficulty: *Easy*
Prep time: *15 min +*
30 min chilling
Baking time: *5 min*

This is not really a recipe but rather an action, that's how quick it is to make these impressive and delicious little sticks. One of Nice's main local products is olives, so we get a really good variety of them. There will always be a type of olive somewhere on the menu. We serve them combined with our bread plate for our guests to snack on while they enjoy a glass of Champagne or South African Méthode Cap Classique. Small, pitted olives are usually the pungent ones and are fantastic with the breadsticks.

INGREDIENTS

Olive and Rosemary Sticks
250 g black pitted olives
4 sprigs rosemary, washed and
stripped
Sea salt and ground black pepper
to taste
280 g puff pastry

Whipped Miso Butter
150 g homemade butter
(see page 142), at room
temperature
10 ml miso paste
Sea salt and ground black pepper

METHOD

For the breadsticks, combine the olives, rosemary, salt and pepper in a blender and mix into a smooth paste. Place the resulting tapenade in a piping bag with a medium-sized nozzle. Roll out the puff pastry into a square shape. Fold in half and then open up again (you do this just to make a mark in the centre). Pipe vertical lines of the tapenade on one half of the pastry, from the middle mark down towards the edge and leaving 3–5 cm between each line. Brush the other half of the pastry using water and a pastry brush. Fold the top half over the piped half and gently press the areas without tapenade so that the pastry sticks together. Use your fingers to run down the tapenade parts to shape them into nice rounds. Place on a tray and freeze until hard.

Meanwhile, make the whipped miso butter. Place the butter and miso paste in a stand mixer and whisk on medium for 10–15 minutes, scraping down the sides from time to time, until light and fluffy. Season to taste with salt and pepper.

Preheat the oven to 200 °C. Remove the pastry from the freezer and leave for a few minutes to soften slightly. Trim the sides and cut the pastry vertically into very thin slices. Place them on a baking tray lined with baking paper and bake in a pre-heated for 5 minutes, or until golden brown. Serve immediately with the whipped miso butter.

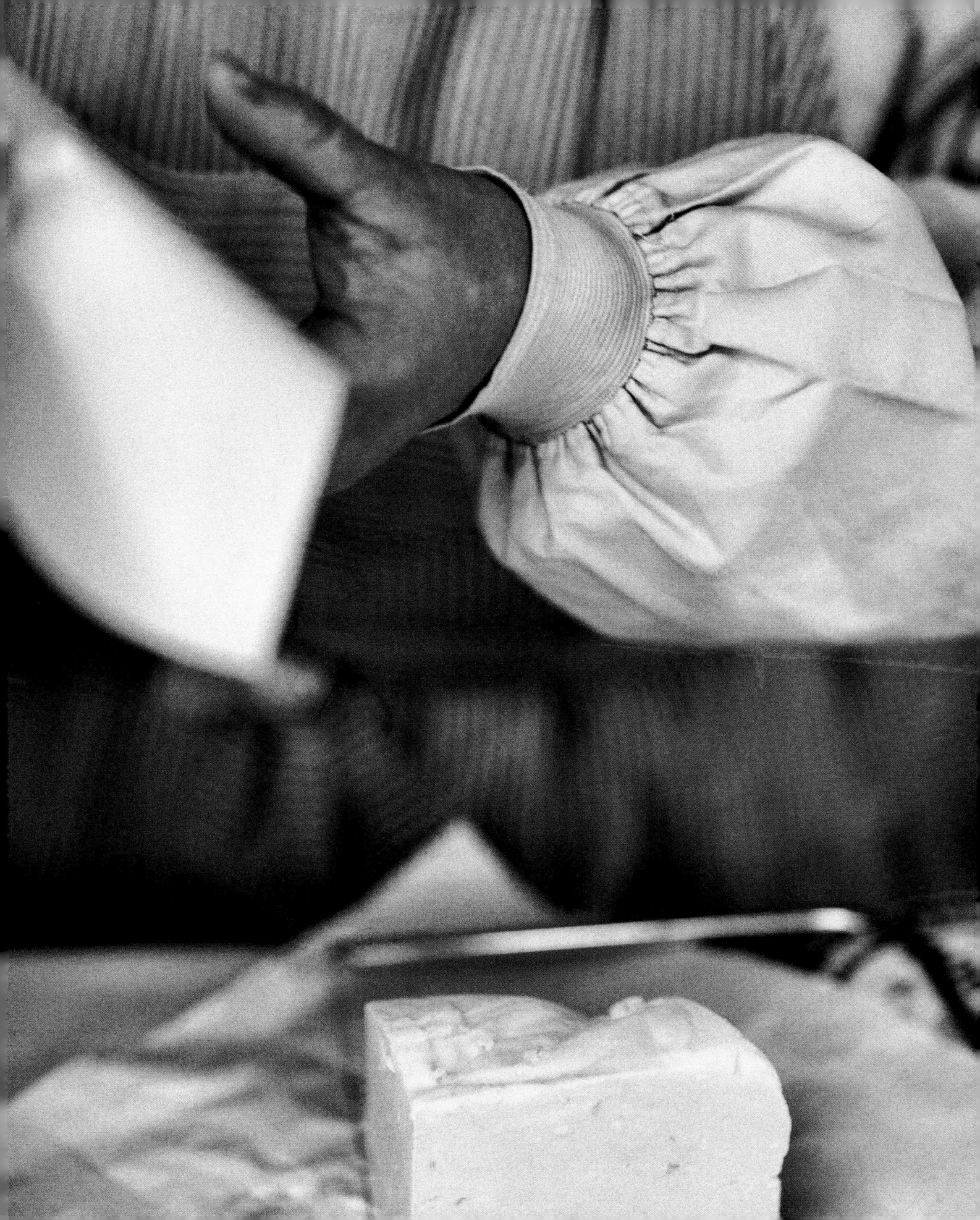

HOMEMADE RICOTTA

Makes: *About 500 g*

Difficulty: *Easy*

Prep time: *1 hr 10 min*

Cooking time: *15 min*

INGREDIENTS

2 L fresh full-cream milk

Peel of 2 lemons, pith removed

30 ml black peppercorns

10 sprigs fresh thyme

10 ml fine salt

Juice of 2 lemons

METHOD

Place the milk, lemon peel, peppercorns, thyme and salt in a large saucepan and bring to the boil. Remove from the heat and set aside to infuse for 30 minutes.

Using a fine-mesh sieve, strain the peel, black peppercorns and thyme. Add the lemon juice to the infused milk, stir gently, then bring to a simmer. Simmer until the milk starts separating into thick curds and clear whey. Be careful not to let it boil as it will break down the curds and spoil your ricotta. Set aside for 5 minutes.

Remove the curd with a slotted spoon and place in a strainer lined with muslin cloth. Leave in the fridge for 30 minutes or longer if you prefer drier ricotta.

HOMEMADE BUTTER

Serves: *About 250 g*
Difficulty: *Easy*
Prep time: *20 min*
Cooking time: *0 min*

INGREDIENTS

500 ml whipping cream or double
cream, at room temperature
Large bowl of ice water
Fine salt to taste

METHOD

Whisk the cream in a stand mixer or jug blender at medium speed until the milk solids start separating from the buttermilk – it will take 5–10 minutes. (You can make larger quantities at a time, just make sure that the bowl is only filled halfway to give enough space for the butter to agitate without splashing out the top or sides.)

Continue whisking until the butter has solidified (takes about 13 minutes), then pour off the buttermilk (save it for baking) and scoop the butter into a bowl.

Rinse the butter by pouring ice water over it and pressing out the remaining buttermilk with a small spatula or spoon. Pour off the water and keep rinsing and squishing the butter with the ice water until the water runs clear. (By removing the buttermilk and squeezing out all the excess liquid you extend the shelf life of the butter, which would otherwise turn rancid quickly.)

Stir in fine salt to taste. Taste as you stir in the salt; you can always add more salt but you can't take it out.

8.

PÂTISSERIE

[ǀpəˈtiːs(ə)ri] (noun) a shop where pastries and cakes are sold,
(mass noun) pastries and cakes collectively

*A French patisserie is the very manifestation of sweet temptation. Found on
nearly every corner, each bakery is renowned for a different baked treat —
dainty millefeuille, chocolate-drenched éclairs, colourful macaroons, dark and
dangerous douceur noisette and a myriad other intricate delicacies.*

*In many ways, baking is so much more involved than cooking. It's not
just butter, sugar and eggs thrown together. You have to be meticulous
in considering the chemistry, beauty and flavours of your creations and
continually challenge yourself by introducing unusual ingredients.*

*At JAN, the cool pastry section of the kitchen is my refuge when the stifling
heat of high summer hits the south of France. It is here that I am reminded
of the singular desserts of my childhood. Surreptitiously dipping a spoon into
some dark ganache or cooling citrus syrup, I am back in my grandmother's
kitchen as a child, stirring French batters with South African spoons.*

APPLE AND CIDER CHARLOTTE

Serves: *6–8*
Difficulty: *Medium*
Prep time: *45 min +*
  2–3 hr chilling
Baking time: *45 min*

INGREDIENTS

1.2 kg Golden Delicious apples,
  peeled, cored and cut into pieces
250 g salted butter
130 g granulated sugar
125 ml water
10 ml vanilla extract
50 g unsalted butter
15 slices brioche, sponge cake or
  white bread/Pain de Mie (see
  page 32)

Cider Caramel
500 ml apple cider
200 g light brown sugar
75 g salted butter
180 ml heavy cream
2.5 ml ground cinnamon
5 ml vanilla extract
Pinch fine sea salt

A charlotte is a type of dessert or trifle that can be served hot or cold. Bread, sponge cake or biscuits are used to line a mould, which is then filled with a fruit purée or custard.

METHOD

Place the apples in a large casserole dish with the salted butter, sugar and water. Cook slowly over moderate heat for 30–40 minutes until a purée forms. Once the purée is smooth, caramelise a little longer on the heat until light golden in colour. Remove from the heat, add the vanilla extract and stir gently.

Preheat the oven to 170 °C. Spray a 20 cm dome-shaped cake tin or a charlotte mould with nonstick spray.

Melt the unsalted butter in a double boiler to form a clarified butter. Slice the bread/sponge into even squares and dip lightly into the clarified butter. Line the base of the cake tin or mould and all around the sides with some of the buttered bread. Make sure there aren't any gaps and that the bread overlaps slightly so that it forms a 'crown' shape. Scoop some of the apple purée onto the base, add a layer of bread and purée and repeat, ending with a layer of bread.

Cover the charlotte with foil and bake for 45 minutes. Take a peek once in a while to check that the crust has gone caramel brown. Set aside until cool and then refrigerate for at least 2–3 hours.

For the cider caramel, pour the apple cider into a medium-sized saucepan and bring to a boil over medium-high heat. Allow the apple cider to cook down to about 80 ml. Reduce the heat and add the brown sugar, butter, cream and cinnamon, and increase the heat back to medium-high. Continue to cook for 10–15 minutes until the caramel thickens and starts to become dark in colour. Remove from the heat, add the vanilla and salt, and stir to combine. Set aside to cool and thicken slightly.

To serve the charlotte, turn the mould upside down on a plate and carefully remove the cake tin. Drizzle over the caramel sauce. Serve with whipped cream or crème fraîche whipped with a little icing sugar.

MILK TART WITH POACHED FRUIT

Serves: *6*

Difficulty: *Medium*

Prep time: *55 min + 2 hr chilling*

Baking time: *20 min*

Cooking time: *40 min*

INGREDIENTS

Sweet Pastry

*125 g cold unsalted butter, cut into
  small cubes*

500 g all-purpose flour, plus extra

30 ml baking powder

Pinch fine salt

125 g icing sugar

*1 vanilla pod, halved and seeds
  scraped out*

1 large egg, beaten

Filling

3 large eggs, separated

1.125 L full-cream milk

80 g cake flour, sifted

65 g cornflour

Pinch salt

110 g granulated sugar

15 ml vanilla extract

2 large egg yolks

*250 g unsalted butter, cut into
  small cubes*

10 ml cinnamon sugar

METHOD

To make the pastry, blend the butter, flour, baking powder, salt and icing sugar in a food processor until the mixture resembles breadcrumbs. Add the vanilla seeds and mix again quickly. Add the egg to the mixture and gently work it together using your hands until you have a ball of dough. Don't overwork the pastry. Sprinkle a little flour over the dough and pat the ball into a flat round about 2.5 cm thick. Sprinkle over a little more flour, then wrap in plastic wrap. Rest in the fridge for at least 30 minutes.

Using a rolling pin, carefully roll out the pastry on a lightly floured work surface until it is about 6 mm thick. Use the rolling pin to lift the pastry and place it into a lightly greased loose-bottomed tart tin. Gently press the pastry onto all the sides and trim off the excess. Prick with a fork and place in the freezer for 30 minutes.

Preheat the oven to 180 °C. Remove the tart shell from the freezer and place a large piece of greaseproof paper inside it. Fill with raw rice or dried beans. Bake blind for 10 minutes, or until lightly browned. Remove the beans and allow to cool.

For the filling, whisk the egg whites until stiff peaks form. Set aside. Mix 125 ml of the milk, the cake flour, cornflour, salt and sugar together until smooth. Bring the remaining milk to just below boiling point, then remove from the heat and stir in the cornflour mixture. Return to the heat, stirring continuously, until the mixture is smooth and thickens. Add the butter, a little at a time, mixing until well combined, then add the vanilla. Beat all the egg yolks lightly and mix into the custard. Gently fold in the whisked egg whites and pour the filling into the baked pastry shell. Bake at 180 °C for 20 minutes and then set aside to cool. Sprinkle with cinnamon sugar.

Serve the milk tart garnished with poached fruit*, Caramel (see page 179) and Caramel Pistachio Tuille (see page 193).

* Muscat-poached pears and quinces: Combine 750 ml muscat, 230 g granulated sugar, 1 cinnamon stick, 5 whole cloves and 1 vanilla pod (halved and seeds scraped out) with the zests of 1 orange and 1 lemon and 500 ml water in a large saucepan. Bring to a boil, then reduce the heat to low and simmer for 10 minutes. Add 5 pears and 5 quinces (all peeled, cored and halved) to the poaching liquid and simmer for 20 minutes, turning them care-fully once with a spoon. Once poached, chill the pears and quinces in the liquid for at least 2 hours and carefully remove with a slotted spoon. Strain the liquid before serving.

LEMON AND POPPY SEED CHEESECAKE

Serves: *8–10*

Difficulty: *Little effort*

Prep time: *40 min +*
2 hr 20 min chilling

Baking time: *25 min*

INGREDIENTS

Lemon and Poppy Seed Cake

7 eggs

460 g sugar

480 g all-purpose flour

15 ml baking powder

310 g butter, melted

80 ml olive oil

Zest of 5 lemons and juice of 1

60 ml poppy seeds

Cheesecake

300 g speculoos biscuits, crushed

30 ml granulated sugar

Zest of 3 lemons

1 cm piece fresh ginger, grated

125 g butter, melted

250 ml fresh cream

500 g cream cheese

250 ml condensed milk

250 ml lemon juice

30 ml vanilla

100 g icing sugar

7 sheets gelatine, soaked in cold
water and drained

METHOD

For the poppy seed cake, preheat the oven to 180 °C. Spray a baking tray with non-stick spray.

In a stand mixer, combine the eggs and sugar and mix until light and fluffy. Sift the flour and baking powder together and fold it into the egg mixture. Mix until well combined.

Combine the melted butter, olive oil, lemon zest and juice and allow to stand for a few minutes before adding it to the flour mixture. Mix until smooth and then add the poppy seeds.

Pour the batter into the prepared tray and bake for 25 minutes, or until the batter is cooked and golden brown. Once cooled, carefully remove from the tray.

Depending on the height of your sponge, trim the top with a large bread knife or use a string to cut it into a perfect flat shape. Set aside.

For the cheesecake, line a medium-sized loaf tin with wax paper and spray with nonstick spray.

Mix the biscuits, sugar, lemon zest, grated ginger and melted butter together in a large mixing bowl. Press a thin layer onto the base of the loaf tin until evenly spread and place in the fridge. Reserve the rest of the mixture at room temperature.

In a stand mixer fitted with the whisk attachment, whisk the cream until thick. Add the cream cheese and whisk on a medium speed until there are no lumps – maximum 2 minutes. Combine the condensed milk, lemon juice, vanilla and icing sugar, add to the cream cheese mixture and whisk lightly.

In a small saucepan, warm the gelatine with some of the leftover water and melt down until smooth – do not boil. Add the gelatine mixture to the cream cheese and cream and whisk for another 2–3 minutes. Be careful not to overmix or it will separate.

Pour a little of the cream cheese filling into the loaf tin on top of the crumble and return to the fridge to set for 20 minutes. Make sure the cheese filling is semi-hard before proceeding with the stacking: add a layer of the sponge, some more cream cheese filling and lastly a layer of biscuit crumbs. Return to the fridge for 2 hours to set.

To serve, roast a few lemons on a griddle pan until they are caramelised and serve with dollops of Caramel (see page 179) and toasted coconut.

BERRIES AND CHOCOLATE

Serves: *6*

Difficulty: *Medium*

Prep time: *45 min +*
30 min chilling

Cooking time: *1 hr*

INGREDIENTS

Chocolate mousse

4 eggs, separated

50 g castor sugar

30 ml cocoa powder

25 ml amaretto

150 ml fresh cream, whisked to
soft peak stage

200 g chocolate, melted

Chocolate Pistachio Tuille

170 g castor sugar

180 g butter

100 ml liquid glucose

60 ml milk

150 g chopped pistachios

30 ml cocoa powder

Garnish

150 g fresh strawberries

50 g ginger biscuits, crumbled

Yoghurt Vanilla Cream

250 g Greek yoghurt

1 vanilla pod, halved lengthways
and scraped

80 g castor sugar

15 ml lemon juice

METHOD

For the chocolate mousse, whisk the egg yolks and sugar in a stand mixer until light and fluffy. Add the cocoa and amaretto. Mix on the lowest setting and add the whipped cream followed by the melted chocolate until mixed through and combined.

Place the egg whites in a large mixing bowl that has been cleaned with vinegar. Whisk at a medium to high speed to fluff them up. Just as they reach soft peak stage remove the whisk. Use a large plastic spoon to combine the egg whites with the rest of the chocolate batter. Whisk a few times to incorporate but don't overmix. Pour the chocolate mousse into a piping bag and place in the fridge until ready to use.

To make the pistachio tuille, heat the sugar, butter, glucose and milk in a medium-sized saucepan over low to medium heat until melted. Increase the heat to high and bring the mixture to a boil. Remove from the heat and add the ground pistachios and cocoa. Mix well before spreading it very thinly on a baking tray lined with baking paper. Press another piece of baking paper on top and smooth out using your hands so that the tuille mixture spreads evenly. Place in the freezer for about 2 hours, or until the mixture is hard.

Preheat the oven to 150 °C. Remove the top layer of baking paper from the frozen tuille and bake in the oven for about 15 minutes. Remove and cool before breaking into pieces as required.

For the yoghurt vanilla cream, use a hand whisk to mix the yoghurt, vanilla seeds, castor sugar and lemon juice together until well combined. Pour into a squeezy bottle and refrigerate for 30 minutes before using.

To assemble the dish, pipe some chocolate mousse in a circle, and add sliced fresh strawberries, Berry Gel (see page 253), yoghurt vanilla cream and the ginger biscuit crumbs. Garnish with pieces of the pistachio tuille.

PEAR AND WHITE CHOCOLATE HAZELNUT CAKE

Serves: 6
Difficulty: *Easy*
Prep time: *40 min*
Baking time: *50–60 min*

INGREDIENTS

100 g hazelnuts, blanched
140 g self-raising flour
175 g butter, cut into small pieces
140 g castor sugar
2 large eggs, beaten
4 medium-sized pears
50 g white chocolate, chopped into
small chunks
30 ml apricot jam

METHOD

Preheat the oven to 140 °C. Butter and line the base of a 20 cm round cake tin.

Grind the hazelnuts in a food processor until fairly fine. Remove 30 ml and set aside. Add the flour to the remaining hazelnuts in the food processor and mix briefly. Add the butter and pulse until it forms crumbs. Add the castor sugar and eggs and mix briefly.

Peel, core and chop two of the pears. Stir the chopped pears and chocolate lightly into the cake mixture using a wooden spoon. Spoon the mixture into the prepared cake tin and smooth the top.

Peel, core and slice the remaining two pears and arrange over the top of the cake. Sprinkle with the reserved chopped hazelnuts. Press down lightly and bake for 50–60 minutes until firm to the touch and golden in colour. Cool in the tin for 10 minutes, then turn out and cool on a wire rack.

Warm the jam and brush over the top of the cake. Dust with icing sugar if desired and serve warm or cold with cream or ice cream.

CRUMBLED CARROT CAKE WITH ORANGE CURD AND HAZELNUT ICE CREAM

Serves: *6*

Difficulty: *Medium*

Prep time: *2 hr (excl churning)*

Cooking time: *about 1 hr*

INGREDIENTS

Hazelnut Ice Cream

375 g hazelnuts, skins on

750 ml full-cream milk

6 large egg yolks

130 g granulated sugar

250 ml cream

15 ml Frangelico liqueur

Carrot Cake

250 g self-raising flour

10 ml ground cinnamon

400 g castor sugar

350 ml vegetable oil

4 eggs

350 g grated carrots

1 ripe banana, puréed

120 g chopped walnuts

Orange Curd

5 oranges

200 g granulated sugar

120 g butter, cut into cubes

2 large eggs, beaten

METHOD

Make the hazelnut ice cream first. Preheat the oven to 180 °C. Spread the hazelnuts on a baking tray and toast in the oven for 8–10 minutes. Cool completely, then rub off the skins, and coarsely grind the nuts in a blender.

Combine the milk and ground hazelnuts in a saucepan over low heat. Bring to a gentle boil, cover, and remove the pan from the heat. Allow to stand for 2 hours. Strain through a fine-mesh sieve or use cheesecloth, pressing hard on the solids to get the liquid to come through. Reserve the strained milk and discard the solids.

Combine the egg yolks and sugar in the bowl of an electric mixer. Cream at medium-high speed for 3–5 minutes until very thick and pale. Return milk to a simmer. Add half of the warm milk to the egg mixture and whisk until blended. Pour the egg yolk mixture into the saucepan with the remaining milk. Cook over low heat, stirring, until the mixture coats the back of a wooden spoon. Remove from the heat and immediately stir in the cream and Frangelico. Pass the mixture through a fine-mesh sieve set over a medium-sized bowl. Place the bowl in an ice-water bath, and cool down. Churn in an ice-cream maker according to the manufacturer's instructions.

For the carrot cake, preheat the oven to 180 °C. Grease two round cake tins of 23 cm in diameter. In a medium-sized bowl, stir the flour, cinnamon and castor sugar together. Add the oil and eggs and mix until blended. Stir in the carrots, banana purée and nuts. Divide the cake mixture evenly between the two prepared tins. Bake for 25–30 minutes, or until a skewer inserted into the cake comes out clean. Cool the cakes on wire racks before removing from the tins.

For the orange curd, soften the oranges by rolling them back and forth on a hard surface, then grate the zest very finely, making sure no white pith is included. Squeeze the juice and combine with the zest, sugar and butter in a medium to large bowl suspended over a pot of boiling water. Mix the sugar and butter until melted. Lower the heat to a simmer. Whisk in the eggs until thickened and the mixture coats the back of a teaspoon. This will take about 20 minutes. Allow to cool before using.

To assemble, break the carrot cake into pieces of different sizes. Serve with dots of Caramel (see page 179), orange curd and Vanilla Yoghurt Cream (see page 155), and a quenelle (see page 54) of the hazelnut ice cream.

CHOCOLATE MOUSSE CAKE WITH ROASTED BANANA

Serves: *6*
Difficulty: *Medium*
Prep time: *45 min + 3 hr chilling*
Cooking time: *30–35 min*

INGREDIENTS

Chocolate Sponge
8 eggs
400 g granulated sugar
30 g butter
60 ml milk
15 ml vanilla extract
100 g all-purpose flour
60 g cocoa powder
5 ml baking powder
Pinch fine salt

Chocolate Mousse
110 g dark chocolate
200 g marshmallows
425 ml evaporated milk, chilled

Roasted Banana Sorbet
4 bananas, unpeeled
60 ml glucose syrup
Pinch fine salt
30 ml rum
375 ml water

Caramelised Banana
3 bananas
100 g granulated sugar

METHOD

For the sponge, preheat the oven to 180 °C. Combine the eggs and sugar in the bowl of an electric mixer fitted with a whisk. Cream at medium-high speed until very thick and pale yellow. Melt the butter in the milk in a heatproof bowl in the microwave or in a small saucepan. Allow to cool down slightly. Slowly mix the milk mixture into the egg mixture and mix on low speed. Add the vanilla extract. Sift the flour, cocoa, baking powder and salt together, add to the egg mixture and combine well. Pour the batter into a buttered oven pan lined with baking paper. Bake for 30–35 minutes, or until a skewer inserted into the sponge comes out clean. Cool and then turn out onto a cooling rack. Cut the chocolate sponge in half horizontally and press into individual moulds or keep as a whole in a cake tin.

For the mousse, break the chocolate into small pieces and melt with the marshmallows and half of the evaporated milk in a double boiler. Stir regularly until smooth. In a separate bowl, whisk the remaining half of the evaporated milk until soft peaks form. Fold into the chocolate mixture and pour onto the individual cakes or into the whole one. Refrigerate for at least 3 hours.

For the roasted banana sorbet, place the bananas – skin and all – on a baking tray and roast in a preheated oven at 160 °C for 20–30 minutes, or until black and syrupy. Remove from the oven and allow to cool. Scoop out the insides of the banana into a blender and add the glucose, salt, rum and water. Blend until smooth and then churn in an ice-cream maker, following the manufacturer's instructions.

For the caramelised banana, use a medium-sized melon baller and scoop out the banana, keeping them as round as possible. Sprinkle with sugar and caramelise using a blowtorch.

To serve, cut the mousse in half and serve with roasted banana sorbet, caramelised banana balls and an individual chocolate tart (see page 168).

SPICY PEAR
SAFFRON TARTE TATIN

Serves: *6–8*
Difficulty: *Easy*
Prep time: *20 min*
Baking time: *30–40 min*

INGREDIENTS

120 g castor sugar

60 g cold butter, cut into cubes

2 pinches saffron

2.5 ml ground ginger

2.5 ml ground cinnamon

*3 large pears, peeled, cored and cut
    into wedges*

1 roll (400 g) puff pastry

METHOD

Preheat the oven to 200 °C. Heat a large ovenproof frying pan over medium heat. Add the castor sugar and stir constantly with a wooden spoon until caramelised. Add the butter, saffron, ginger and cinnamon and stir to combine.

Place the pears in the caramel and spoon over some of the caramel. Turn the heat down and cook for 5–10 minutes, until the pears are just tender and cooked but retain their shape. Remove from the heat and cool slightly. Re-arrange in a fan shape in the pan.

Roll out the pastry to about 5 mm thick and cut a disc slightly bigger than the pan. Place the pastry disc on top of the pears and caramel, then carefully tuck it snugly around the outside of the pears and down into the sides of the pan.

Bake the tarte Tatin for 30–40 minutes, or until the pastry is golden brown and puffed up. Remove from the oven and leave for 10 minutes to cool down. Loosen the pastry by running a knife around the edge, then place a large serving plate over the top and carefully turn over onto the plate. Serve warm with cream or custard.

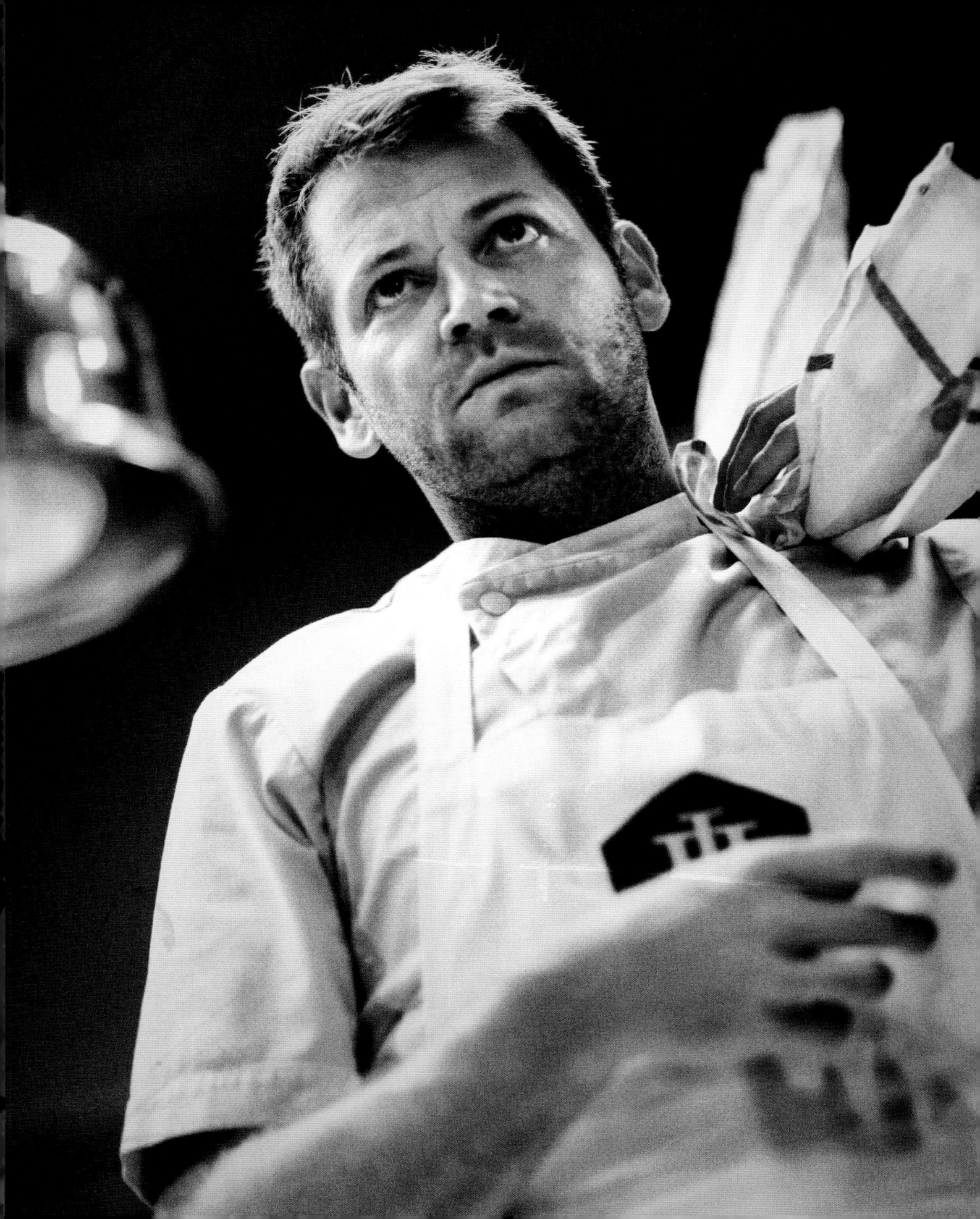

CHOCOLATE AND CASSIS TART

Makes: *2 medium tarts*
Difficulty: *Medium*
Prep time: *2 hr*
Cooking time: *1 hr*

INGREDIENTS

1 batch Sweet Pastry (see
page 149)

Chocolate Filling
250 g dark chocolate
50 g butter
120 g granulated sugar
200 ml fresh cream
5 ml fine salt
4 eggs
1 vanilla pod, halved and seeds
scraped out

Cassis Berries
450 g cassis or blackberries
100 g granulated sugar
80 ml crème de cassis
80 ml water
10 ml lemon zest

The cassis berries can be substituted with blackberries or mulberries. When soaked in the cassis,
the liqueur of the South of France, it adds a tangy but sweet, deep flavour.

METHOD

Preheat the oven to 180 °C. Use a loose-bottomed tart tin and, using a splash of vegetable oil on a piece of paper towel, lightly oil the inside.

Prepare the pastry, wrap in plastic wrap and allow to rest in the fridge for at least 30 minutes before using.

Roll out the pastry on a lightly floured work surface until it is about 6 mm thick. Use the rolling pin to lift the pastry and place it into the tart tin. Gently press the pastry onto all the sides and trim off the excess. Prick with a fork and place in the freezer for 30 minutes.

Preheat the oven to 180 °C. Remove the tart shell from the freezer and place a large piece of greaseproof paper inside. Fill with raw rice or dried beans. Bake blind for 10 minutes, then remove the beans and bake a second time until lightly browned. Remove and allow to cool.

For the filling, melt the chocolate and butter in a double boiler or on a medium setting in the microwave. Stir regularly to prevent the chocolate from burning. Allow to stand for 10 minutes to thicken.

In the bowl of an electric mixer fitted with the whisk attachment, whisk the sugar, cream, salt, eggs and vanilla seeds until smooth. Add the chocolate and butter mixture and mix well. Pour the filling into the tart shell and bake at 180 °C for 15–20 minutes – it should still be slightly wobbly. Remove from the oven and allow to cool completely before removing from the tart tin.

For the cassis berries, wash the berries and place half of them in a small saucepan with the sugar, crème de cassis, water and lemon zest. Simmer until it forms a syrup. Just before serving, mix in the remaining berries and give it a good stir. Allow to rest for 10 minutes before spooning on top of the chocolate tart.

TIRAMISU

Serves: *10*
Difficulty: *Little effort*
Prep time: *40 min*
Baking time: *20–25 min*

INGREDIENTS

Vanilla Sponge

7 eggs
460 g castor sugar
480 g all-purpose flour
15 ml baking powder
300 g butter, melted
80 ml canola oil
15 ml vanilla extract
1 vanilla pod, halved lengthways
  and scraped

Chocolate Sponge

See page 162

Tiramisu Filling

50 ml fresh cream
250 g cream cheese
70 g castor sugar
1 vanilla pod, halved lengthways
  and scraped

250 ml strong coffee / espresso
Cocoa powder for dusting

Because Nice was Italian in its early days and called Nizza, the Italian influence is still present, especially in favourites such as tiramisu. It is served with coffee ice cream or plain vanilla ice cream and a strong shot of espresso. Bellissimo!

METHOD

Preheat the oven to 180 °C.

To make the vanilla sponge, beat the eggs and castor sugar together until light and fluffy. Sift in the flour and baking powder and mix until just combined. Add the butter, oil and vanilla extract and seeds and mix well. Pour the batter into a buttered oven pan lined with baking paper. Bake for 20–25 minutes. Set aside to cool.

For the filling, whisk the cream to soft peak stage and then add the cream cheese, castor sugar and vanilla seeds. Whisk until smooth and creamy.

To assemble, cut the vanilla sponge and wet slightly with the coffee. Layer the vanilla and cut chocolate sponges in individual bowls or glasses with the cream cheese filling and top with a dusting of cocoa powder. Allow to stand for a few hours for the flavours to develop.

MELON AND ORANGE GRANITA

Serves: *6*

Difficulty: *Easy*

Prep time: *15 min + 5 hr chilling*

Cooking time: *0 min*

INGREDIENTS

500 ml fresh orange juice

100 g granulated sugar

30 ml white balsamic vinegar

1 vanilla pod, cut in half and seeds
  scraped out

2 sweet melons

METHOD

Combine 250 ml orange juice, the sugar, white balsamic vinegar and vanilla pod with seeds in a small saucepan and boil over high heat for about 1 minute, stirring until the sugar dissolves. Cut the melons in half, clean out the seeds and remove the skin. Cut into big chunks and place in a food processor with the remaining 250 ml orange juice and the warm sugar/orange mixture. Blend on medium speed for 10 minutes, or until smooth. Transfer the mixture to a shallow dish and freeze, scraping around the sides every 30 minutes to break up the crystals. Cover with plastic wrap until ready to serve.

9.

MIGNARDISE

[/miɲaʁdiz/] (plural mignardises) a bite-sized
dessert, sometimes served at the end of a meal

*These little sweet treats are the perfect way to remind our guests
of our unique South African heritage and showcase the tastes and
textures of my childhood. Normally served alongside some piping
hot rooibos tea or a shot of my father's potent home-distilled
peach mampoer as digestif, our mignardises often feature radical
re-imaginings of traditional South African favourites such as milk
tart, malva pudding, Hertzoggies and more.When JAN first opened
it was likely the only restaurant in the south of France to serve
malva and koesisters, but the recipe has since been begged, borrowed
and wheedled by locals to the point where it probably graces more
French tea trays than we will ever know.*

CHOCOLATE BARK

Serves: *about 36 blocks*

Difficulty: *Easy*

Prep time: *15 min + 2 hr chilling*

Cooking time: *0 min*

INGREDIENTS

400 g dark chocolate chips

30 ml butter

*397 g (1 can) sweetened
    condensed milk*

5 ml vanilla extract

METHOD

Line a 20 cm square cake tin with foil and spray lightly with nonstick spray. Set aside.

In a microwave-safe bowl, microwave the chocolate chips and butter together on high for 1 minute. Rest for 1 minute and then check to see if it has melted. If necessary, microwave for another 30–45 seconds. Stir the chocolate until all the lumps are gone.

Stir in the condensed milk and vanilla. Once completely incorporated, press the mixture into the prepared cake tin. Refrigerate for a minimum of 2 hours to set before cutting into squares — pull a fork through the chocolate before it has set completely to give it the appearance of bark. Cut into squares and store in an airtight container.

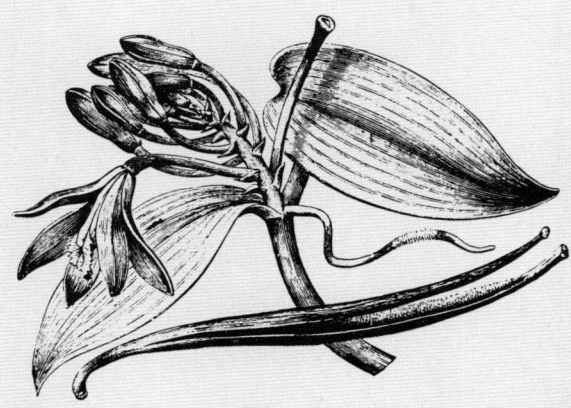

MILK TART
CROQUEMBOUCHE

Serves: *8–10*

Difficulty: *Medium*

Preparation time: *15 min*

Baking time: *20–25 min*

INGREDIENTS

1 batch milk tart filling

  (see page 149)

Ground cinnamon to taste

Pastry Puffs

100 g unsalted butter

375 ml water

1 ml fine salt

5 ml sugar

225 g sifted all-purpose flour

7 large eggs

Caramel

160 ml water

400 g granulated sugar

A glamorous French dessert, literally meaning crunch in the mouth, and very often served as an Italian wedding cake.

METHOD

Preheat the oven to 220 °C. Line a baking tray with baking paper.

To make the puffs, place the butter, water, salt and sugar in a medium-sized saucepan and heat until the butter has melted. Remove from the heat and add the flour.

Return the saucepan to the heat and, using a wooden spoon, beat vigorously for 2–3 minutes. Cool slightly, then add 6 eggs, one at a time, beating vigorously. Transfer the mixture to a pastry bag fitted with a plain nozzle.

Make a glaze by beating the remaining egg with 5 ml water, and set aside.

Pipe out mounds that are 2.5 cm high and 2 cm in diameter on the prepared baking tray. Brush with egg glaze and smooth the tops. Bake for 20–25 minutes until puffed and golden. Cool on wire racks.

Mix the ground cinnamon into the milk tart filling. Once the puffs are cooled, cut a small opening in the bottom of each puff and fill with warm milk tart filling.

To make the caramel, combine the water and sugar in a medium-sized saucepan and bring to a boil over high heat. Do not stir. Cover the saucepan and boil until the steam dissolves any crystals. Uncover and boil for 5 minutes more, or until the syrup is amber in colour. Remove from the heat. Dip the bottom of each puff into the caramel, and then arrange the puffs in a pyramid. Drizzle the leftover caramel over the top.

BURNT BUTTER, HONEY AND BUCHU MADELEINES

Serves: *36 small or 16 large*

Difficulty: *Medium*

Preparation time: *30 min*

Baking time: *5–10 min*

INGREDIENTS

140 g salted butter

20 g dried buchu leaves

3 eggs

80 g granulated sugar

45 ml honey

150 g all-purpose flour

60 ml cornflour

5 ml baking powder

Pinch fine salt

Two key factors: cold batter and a hot oven!

METHOD

Preheat the oven to 180 °C. Grease a madeleine pan with nonstick spray.

In a small saucepan, melt the butter over low heat until it becomes brown in colour. Remove from heat, add the buchu and allow to infuse for at least 10 minutes, then strain.

Mix the eggs and sugar in a stand mixer until very fluffy. Add the honey and mix until combined. Sift in the flour, cornflour, baking powder and salt. Mix on slow speed until well combined, then slowly add the burnt butter mixture. Fill the moulds in the prepared pan to just below half. Bake the madeleines for 5–10 minutes, or until golden brown.

MALVA TRUFFLES WITH SMOKED ROSEMARY

Makes: *about 60*

Difficulty: *Little effort*

Prep time: *30 min + 1 hr chilling*

Baking time: *20–25 min*

INGREDIENTS

Truffles

400 g sugar

4 eggs

90 ml apricot jam

375 g all-purpose flour

Pinch fine salt

10 ml bicarbonate of soda

30 ml butter

250 ml milk

30 ml white vinegar

30 ml vanilla extract

Sauce

500 ml milk

250 ml fresh cream

250 ml water

30 ml butter

30 ml vanilla extract

200 g sugar

250 g milk chocolate, melted

1 sprig fresh rosemary per truffle
  for serving

METHOD

Preheat the oven to 180 °C. Butter a 65 cm x 30 cm oven pan generously and line the bottom with wax paper.

For the truffles, beat the sugar, eggs and jam together in a stand mixer on medium speed until pale and fluffy. Sift in the flour, salt and bicarbonate of soda and mix well. Melt the butter in the milk. Add the vinegar and vanilla to the egg mixture and slowly add the butter and milk to the batter. Mix until completely blended.

Pour the batter into the prepared pan and bake for 20–25 minutes until the pudding begins to pull away from the sides of the dish and a toothpick inserted in the centre of the pudding comes out clean.

Combine the sauce ingredients in a saucepan and heat only long enough to melt the butter. Pour the sauce over the pudding as soon as it comes out of the oven, and allow it to be absorbed. Let the pudding rest and cool down, then refrigerate for at least 1 hour.

Scoop out a full teaspoon of the pudding and place in the palm of your hand. Roll gently into a ball. Skewer the ball onto a sprig of rosemary and dip into the melted chocolate, then place on a drip tray to harden. If you want to be fancy, use a blowtorch and smoke the rosemary right before serving or in front of your guests as we do at JAN.

RASPBERRY AND CREAM MERINGUE KISSES

Makes: *30*
Difficulty: *Medium*
Prep time: *30 min*
Baking time: *1 hr*

INGREDIENTS

4 egg whites

230 g castor sugar

15 ml rose-water

Few drops red food colouring
   (optional)

Raspberry Cream

300 ml cream

15 ml icing sugar, sifted

100 g fresh raspberries or thawed
   frozen raspberries

METHOD

Preheat the oven to 120 °C. Line two baking trays with baking paper and mark 30 circles measuring 3 cm in diameter on each sheet of paper.

Beat the egg whites in a large bowl with an electric beater until stiff peaks form. Add the sugar gradually, beating well after each addition. Continue until thick and glossy. Add the rose-water and food colouring if using to tint the meringue pink.

Transfer the mixture, in batches if needed, into a piping bag fitted with a 1 cm plain nozzle. Following the marked rounds as a guide, pipe the meringue onto the paper. Bake for 1 hour. Leave to cool in the switched-off oven with the oven door slightly ajar.

In a separate bowl, beat the cream and icing sugar until thick, and then fold in the raspberries. Spread the raspberry cream over the base of half the meringues and sandwich with the remaining meringues. Store any unfilled meringues in an airtight container.

NAARTJIE PANNA COTTA WITH WHITE CHOCOLATE ROCKS

Makes: *12 medium-sized glasses*
Difficulty: *Easy*
Prep time: *30 min + 2 hr chilling*
Cooking time: *10 min*

INGREDIENTS

1 L cream
300 ml milk
400 g granulated sugar
Zest and juice of 2 naartjies
Zest and juice of 2 lemons
8 leaves gelatine

Rice Krispies and White
   Chocolate Rocks
200 g white chocolate,
   broken into pieces
125 g Rice Krispies
50 g desiccated coconut

METHOD

Place the cream, milk, sugar and the juice and zests of the naartjies and lemons (reserve some of the naartjie zest for garnishing) in a large saucepan over medium heat and stir until well combined. Soften the gelatine leaves in cold water, then mix into the milk and cream and whisk gently until the gelatine has melted. Use individual glasses of your choice and pour in the mixture until it reaches just above halfway. Refrigerate for 2 hours until set.

For the rocks, melt the chocolate in a saucepan over low heat (or in a bowl in the microwave). Remove from the heat and stir in the Rice Krispies and coconut. Spoon the mixture into small rock shapes, sprinkle with naartjie zest and leave to cool.

To serve, garnish the panna cottas with flower petals and top each one with a chocolate rock.

CARAMEL AND PISTACHIO TUILLE

Makes: *2 standard baking pans*
Difficulty: *Easy*
Prep time: *30 min*
Baking time: *10 min*

INGREDIENTS

85 g granulated sugar

90 g butter

45 ml liquid glucose

50 ml milk

100 g shelled and ground
pistachios

METHOD

Place all the ingredients, except the pistachios, in a saucepan and heat slowly until melted. Increase the heat and bring to a boil. The tuille batter needs to be caramelised. Remove from the heat and add the pistachios. Pour some of the tuille mix in between two sheets of wax paper and roll out with a rolling pin until flat and about 5 mm thick. Place on two baking trays in the freezer and freeze until hard.

Preheat the oven to 150 °C. Remove the trays from the freezer and bake the tuilles for about 10 minutes until crisp. Allow to cool and then break into pieces.

FRUIT PASTELS

Makes: *about 50*

Difficulty: *Medium*

Prep time: *15 min +*
overnight setting

Cooking time: *55 min*

INGREDIENTS

800 g high pectin fruit (such as
apples, guavas, quince, plums,
oranges or pears), washed and
roughly chopped, pips reserved

125 ml apple juice

180 ml liquid glucose

300 g jam sugar (pectin sugar)

110 g castor sugar for coating

METHOD

Line a 21 cm x 14 cm baking tray with a double layer of plastic wrap. (Wet the tray and wipe the plastic wrap with a wet cloth to help it stick to the tray.)

Place the fruit, stones/pips and apple juice in a saucepan and bring to a boil. Reduce heat to low and simmer for about 30 minutes until the fruit is soft. Strain the fruit through a fine-mesh sieve and measure out about 500 ml. Place in a clean saucepan and add the liquid glucose. Bring to a boil, then reduce the heat and simmer for 10–15 minutes, or until the mixture reaches a temperature of 105 °C. Stir occasionally to prevent it from catching.

Add the jam sugar and stir over low heat until the sugar has dissolved completely. Turn up the heat and bring to a boil. Cook for 10 minutes, or until it reaches 105 °C for the second time. Immediately pour the mixture into the prepared tray and set aside to cool and set overnight.

Cut into 1.5 cm squares and roll in the castor sugar. Store in an airtight container for 2–3 days. You can store them without the sugar coating in an airtight container in the fridge for up to a month.

FIG ROCKY ROAD

Makes: *40*
Difficulty: *Easy*
Prep time: *35 min + 2 hr chilling*
Cooking time: *0 min*

INGREDIENTS

*250 g white and pink
    marshmallows, halved*
80 g cashew nuts, roughly chopped
80 g flaked almonds
*110 g fresh figs, quartered (and
    peeled if preferred)*
60 g desiccated coconut
175 g dark chocolate, chopped
175 g milk chocolate, chopped
*50 g roughly chopped hazelnuts,
    toasted*
30 ml Nutella®

METHOD

Line the base and the sides of a 20 cm square cake tin with baking paper.

Place the marshmallows, cashew nuts, almonds, figs and coconut in a large bowl and mix until well combined.

Place the chocolate in a heatproof bowl suspended over a saucepan of simmering water, ensuring the bowl doesn't touch the water. Stir occasionally until the chocolate is just melted and smooth. After the chocolate has cooled, add it to the marshmallow mixture along with the hazelnuts and Nutella, and toss until well combined. Spoon the mixture into the prepared tin and press evenly over the base. Refrigerate for several hours, or until set.

Carefully lift out of the tin, peel away the paper and cut into small pieces. Store in an airtight container in the fridge for up to one week.

10.

L'EQUIPE

[ekipe] team. Feminine *équipée*

While a restaurant's main aim is to delight and regale its diners, and time remains of the essence from the moment we unlock in the morning until we leave at night, we do have to stop and consider feeding the team that runs the show behind the scenes. Delicious, nutritious staff meals are the best way to ensure that your team is properly energised and inspired to tackle the busy shift ahead.

At JAN our chefs' dinners vary greatly from day to day. It is the perfect opportunity to use surplus ingredients, make space in the fridge for newly delivered produce or test-drive a new recipe, and we try to treat ourselves with something special quite often. These meals are enjoyed as a family. We sit down to talk about the previous evening's service, discuss the evening ahead and grow quiet in the face of the new day's challenge, much like warriors approaching the line. And then we dig in!

TEMPURA COURGETTE FLOWERS STUFFED WITH ZESTY RICOTTA

Serves: *8*
Difficulty: *Easy*
Prep time: *30 min*
Cooking time: *10 min*

INGREDIENTS

220 g Homemade Ricotta (see
* page 141)*
Zest and juice of 1–2 lemons
1 clove garlic, crushed
Sea salt and ground black pepper
16 courgette flowers, tips trimmed
* and washed*

Batter
120 g cornflour
Large pinch fine salt
125 ml sparkling water
Vegetable oil for deep-frying

METHOD

Mix the ricotta, lemon zest, lemon juice and garlic together and season well. Pipe or spoon the filling into the courgette flowers. Gently twist the tips of the flowers to seal in the filling.

For the batter, place the cornflour and salt in a large bowl. Slowly add the sparkling water while whisking.

Heat a saucepan filled a third of the way with oil over medium-high heat. (Test the oil by frying a piece of bread; if the bread turns golden within 30 seconds, the oil is ready.)

Dip the flowers in the batter and fry a few at a time for 5–8 minutes, or until golden and crispy. Repeat with the rest of the flowers. Serve immediately.

POACHED PEAR AND BLOOD ORANGE SALAD WITH GOAT'S CHEESE

Serves: *6*
Difficulty: *Medium*
Prep time: *15 min*
Cooking time: *20 min*

INGREDIENTS

Pear and Blood Orange Salad

250 ml water

300 g granulated sugar

1 cinnamon stick

2 blood oranges, cut into eighths

1 lemon, ends cut off, cut into eighths

6 baby onions, halved crossways

Extra virgin olive oil for drizzling

Sea salt and ground black pepper

3 big handfuls rocket leaves, washed

3 pears, quartered and poached
   (see page 149)

75 g raisins

250 g goat's cheese or optional
   blue cheese, sliced

Dressing

30 ml orange juice

15 ml lemon juice

5 ml Dijon mustard

5 ml honey

1 ml fresh thyme, picked

60 ml extra virgin olive oil

METHOD

To make the salad, bring the water, sugar and cinnamon stick to a simmer in a medium-sized saucepan. Stir only until the sugar has dissolved. Gently slide the oranges and lemon slices into the syrup and press down until they are completely submerged. If the fruit keeps floating to the surface, use a heatproof plate as a weight. Simmer gently for 20 minutes, or until the edges of the citrus become translucent. Remove with a slotted spoon and place on a drip tray to cool down before using.

Preheat the oven to 180 °C. Line a baking tray with foil and spread out the onions in a single layer. Sprinkle with olive oil and seasoning and toss lightly so that the onions are coated evenly with oil and seasoning. Roast for 20–25 minutes until slightly browned and tender. Set aside to cool slightly.

For the dressing, combine the orange juice, lemon juice, mustard, honey and thyme in a small bowl. Gradually whisk in the oil, season to taste and set aside.

To assemble the salad, toss the rocket in a large bowl with some of the dressing, then add the oranges, pears, raisins and onions. Divide between six plates and arrange the goat's cheese on top. Garnish with melba toast and drizzle with the remaining dressing.

FRENCH BEAN, GRAPE AND HAZELNUT SALAD WITH GRAPEFRUIT

Serves: 6

Difficulty: *Easy*

Prep time: *1 hr*

Cooking time: *0 min*

INGREDIENTS

400 g French beans

200 g dragon tongue romano beans
  or Mange tout

60 ml extra virgin olive oil

1 clove garlic, crushed

30 ml hazelnut oil

15 ml raspberry vinegar

Small bunch fresh chives or dill

15 ml honey

Fine sea salt and ground black
  pepper

100 g unskinned hazelnuts, toasted

80 g black seedless grapes

80 g white seedless grapes

1 grapefruit

This is a summer favourite — unpretentious bites of sweet, juicy grapes with toasty hazelnuts. It's also great for making in advance as the dressing gets soaked up by the beans.

METHOD

Blanch the French beans and the dragon tongue beans quickly in salted boiling water. Refresh in ice water and set aside. Mix the olive oil, garlic, hazelnut oil, raspberry vinegar, chives and honey in a blender and season with salt and pepper.

In a large mixing bowl, combine the beans, toasted hazelnuts and grapes with the juice of half the grapefruit. Pour over the dressing and toss the salad. Slice the remaining half of the grapefruit and use to garnish the salad.

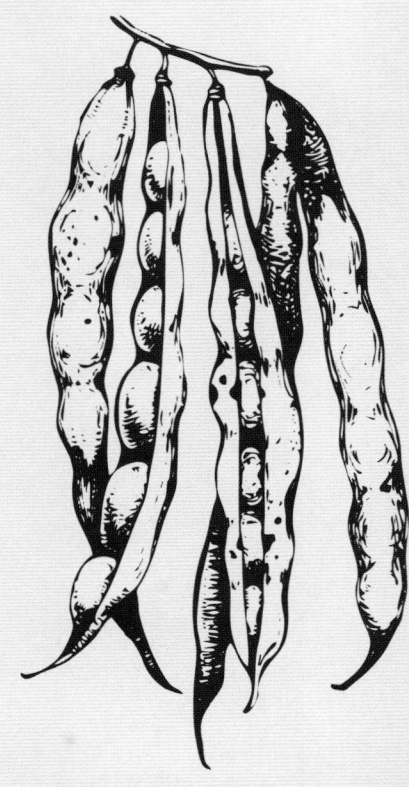

POT-AU-FEU

Serves: *6*

Difficulty: *Easy*

Prep time: *30 min + overnight chilling*

Preparation time: *3–4 hr*

INGREDIENTS

100 ml extra virgin olive oil

1.3 kg beef (preferably cheek, otherwise shank or brisket)

6 large carrots, peeled, plus 1 for the stock, peeled and quartered

1 large onion, studded with cloves

1 clove garlic, with skin left on

1 long stalk celery, quartered

1 bouquet garni (see page 44), including parsley, bay leaf and thyme

Small handful peppercorns

4 leeks, halved if small or quartered if large

Sea salt and ground black pepper

6 turnips, peeled and cut into wedges

1 head cabbage, cored and cut into wedges

6 beef marrowbones per person

Prepare this dish one day in advance to leave time for degreasing.

METHOD

Heat the olive oil in a large saucepan and sear the beef until brown on both sides. Add the quartered carrots, onion, garlic, celery, bouquet garni, peppercorns, salt and some of the green bits of the leeks. Fill with water and cover. Bring to a simmer and cook over medium heat for around 3 hours. While it's simmering, check frequently and use a spoon to skim off any impurities and grease from the top. Leave to cool and place in the fridge overnight.

The next day, scrape off the layer of grease that has formed on the surface. Place the saucepan back on the stove over low heat and put a steamer on top of the saucepan. Place the remaining carrots and the turnips in the steamer and cook for about 15 minutes. Add the cabbage and the remaining leeks and cook for another 10–15 minutes but do not overcook – the vegetables should be firm.

Dab the ends of the beef marrowbones in salt and wrap each piece in aluminium foil. Fill a large saucepan with water and set over high heat. Add salt and pepper when the water is boiling, then add the marrowbones and bring down to a simmer for 10 minutes.

Remove the garlic and the bouquet garni. Serve the meat and marrowbones in one dish and the vegetables in another, with the bouillon on the side. Serve gherkins and wholegrain mustard on the side.

EVERYONE'S FAVOURITE SPAGHETTI BOLOGNESE

Serves: *4–6*
Difficulty: *Easy*
Prep time: *20 min*
Cooking time: *40 min*

INGREDIENTS

60 ml vegetable oil

2 onions, finely chopped

3 cloves garlic, minced

125 g streaky bacon, chopped

4 medium-sized carrots, finely chopped

4 stalks celery, finely chopped

30 ml tomato paste

2 cans (440 g each) whole peeled tomatoes

45 ml apricot jam

3 good splashes of red Tabasco sauce

5 ml paprika

250 ml red wine

250 ml port

45 ml raspberry vinegar

1 kg beef mince

1 sprig fresh rosemary

1 L Chicken Stock (see page 249)

500 g spaghetti

METHOD

Heat the oil in a large saucepan over medium heat. Sauté the onions, garlic and bacon until golden. Add the carrots and celery and sauté until caramelised.

Add the tomato paste, whole peeled tomatoes, jam, Tabasco and paprika, and cook for 5 minutes, or until thickened. Deglaze the saucepan with the red wine, port and vinegar. Stir through the beef and rosemary, add the stock and simmer for 40 minutes, or until cooked and luscious.

To make the spaghetti, bring a large saucepan of salted water to a boil. Add the spaghetti and cook for 6–8 minutes, or until *al dente*.

Divide the spaghetti between bowls and ladle the bolognaise sauce over the top. Serve with shaved pecorino and a handful of chopped parsley.

PORK CHOPS WITH WHISKEY-SOAKED FIGS

Serves: *4*

Difficulty: *Medium*

Prep time: *30 min + 1 hr soaking*

Cooking time: *10 mins*

INGREDIENTS

100 ml whiskey

4 dried figs

60 g butter

4 thick pork chops

2.5 ml fine salt

2.5 ml ground black pepper

150 g apricot jam

4 sprigs fresh rosemary, leaves
picked

4 fresh figs, halved

You don't have to soak the figs in whiskey, but if you like that kind of thing it's a beautiful combination.

METHOD

Heat the whiskey in a small saucepan to just below boiling point. Soak the dried figs in the whiskey in a small bowl for about 1 hour.

Preheat the oven to 160 °C.

Melt the butter in a large pan until sizzling, then add the pork chops and cook over medium-high heat, turning once. Season with salt and pepper then remove and set aside.

Use the leftover whiskey to deglaze the pan and add the apricot jam and rosemary to form a sticky sauce. Cover the pork chops with the sauce and place the figs in between the chops, well spaced out. Bake for 10 minutes. Serve with the fresh figs.

FOCCACIA

Serves: *10*
Difficulty: *Easy*
Prep time: *15 min + 1 hr proving*
Cooking time: *20 minutes*

Have fun with the toppings and be sure to eat the focaccia almost immediately once out of the oven. Options for the topping can vary from rosemary, garlic and anchovies to tomato and basil or balsamic onions.

INGREDIENTS

*400 g strong white bread flour,
   plus extra*
*100 g fine semolina flour or strong
   white bread flour*
2.5 ml fine sea salt
1 sachet (10 g) instant yeast
15–30 ml golden castor sugar
300 ml lukewarm water
Extra virgin olive oil
Few sprigs fresh rosemary
6 cloves garlic, peeled
Anchovies
Tomato purée (optional)
Ground black pepper

METHOD

Place both flours and the sea salt in a large bowl. Make a well in the centre. In a separate bowl or jug, mix the yeast, castor sugar and water together with a fork. Set aside for a few minutes. When the yeast mixture starts to foam, pour it slowly into the well in the flour and mix with a fork as you go. As soon as all the ingredients come together, which may take a minute or so, knead vigorously for around 5 minutes until you have a smooth, springy, soft dough.

Lightly oil a large bowl with some olive oil and transfer the dough to the bowl. Dust with a little extra flour, cover with a tea towel and leave to prove in a warm place for 30 minutes until doubled in size.

As soon as the dough has risen, knock it back, then place on a baking tray and spread it out to cover the tray. Push down roughly on top of the dough with your fingertips to make lots of dips and wells. Top with the rosemary, garlic and anchovies or any topping you prefer. Season well with salt and ground black pepper and leave to prove for another 20 minutes. While the dough is rising, preheat the oven to 200 °C.

Bake for 20 minutes until golden on top and soft in the centre.

BAKED PARMESAN COURGETTE FRIES

Serves: *8–10*
Difficulty: *Easy*
Prep time: *30 min*
Cooking time: *20 min*

Summer gives us an abundance of green and yellow courgettes and we can't help but use a few to make these delicious fries for the team. A dash of garlic, lemon cream or a fresh basil and toasted pine nut pesto makes them gorgeous!

INGREDIENTS

8 medium yellow or green
   courgettes
180 g Panko breadcrumbs
90 g Parmesan cheese, grated
5 ml fine sea salt
5 ml ground black pepper
30 ml lemon zest
4 eggs, beaten

METHOD

Preheat the oven to 220 °C. Cut the courgettes lengthways into 10 mm thick spears. In a large mixing bowl, mix the Panko breadcrumbs, Parmesan cheese, salt, pepper and lemon zest.

Dip the courgette sticks into the beaten eggs and then roll in the breadcrumb mixture to coat evenly. Spray a baking tray with nonstick spray and place the courgette sticks on the tray.

Bake for 10 minutes, then turn them around and bake for another 10 minutes until crisp and browned. Garnish with fresh parsley.

ROASTED BANANA, RUM AND RAISIN RICE CAKE (GÂTEAU DE RIZ)

Serves: *8–10*
Difficulty: *Medium*
Prep time: *1 hr*
Baking time: *1 hr*

This very old recipe makes a deliciously creamy but cake-like rice pudding. We usually make this for the crew on Saturday evenings, not only to put a smile on everyone's face just before service, but also so that they can take some home for the weekend.

INGREDIENTS

60 g raisins

60 ml dark rum

1.5 L full-cream milk

200 g short grain white rice, such as Italian arborio

300 g plus 15 ml granulated sugar

1 vanilla pod, split lengthways

5 ml fine salt

4 eggs, separated

30 ml apricot jam

2 bananas, halved

15 ml granulated sugar

5 ml water

METHOD

Soak the raisins in the rum in a bowl for 1 hour.

Combine the milk, rice, 100 g of the sugar, the vanilla pod and salt in a medium-sized saucepan. Bring to a boil over medium heat. Reduce heat to medium-low and cook for about 1 hour until the rice absorbs the liquid. Stir occasionally. Remove from the heat. Scrape the vanilla seeds into the rice and discard the pod. Set aside to cool to room temperature.

Pour 200 g of sugar into a large saucepan, shaking the pan so that the sugar coats the bottom of the pan evenly. Place over medium-high heat and cook for about 2 minutes without stirring until the sugar begins to melt. Now stir with a wooden spoon until golden and just beginning to foam. Remove from the heat and carefully pour into a cake tin. Work fast before the caramel sets, tilting the pan sideways to coat the bottom and sides.

Preheat the oven to 160 °C. Stir the egg yolks, raisins (discard the rum) and apricot jam into the rice. Beat the egg whites until foamy. Sprinkle in the remaining 15 ml sugar and continue to beat until soft peaks form. Fold the egg whites into the rice mixture. Transfer to the caramelised tin, set the tin in a shallow pan of water and bake for about 1 hour until a knife inserted into the centre comes out clean. Cool slightly in the tin, then turn out onto a platter.

Caramelise the bananas in a hot frying pan with the sugar and water. Garnish the cake with the roasted bananas and serve with custard.

11.

APRÈS MINUIT

[ah-PREH mee-NWEE] after midnight

There seems to be a widespread assumption that every meal a chef sits down to eat is prepared carefully, plated beautifully and savoured slowly. Au contraire, mon ami! In fact, we spend so much time ensuring that our guests are well fed that we often only sit down to eat around midnight, after the kitchen has been put to rights and everything is ready and prepped for the next day. This is when we take sneaky little shortcuts and follow our gut to create easy, unfussy dishes to enjoy alongside that well-deserved drink after a long service. The dishes in this chapter are the result of these late night forays into the freezer and can be used to serve two peckish folks or one ravenous human. Here's to easy, unpretentious, yet lovingly prepared midnight snacks! Enjoy!

RED, GREEN AND
YELLOW PICKLED SALADS

GIFT
IDEA

INGREDIENTS

Basic Pickling Liquid*

50 g granulated sugar

150 ml vinegar of choice

150 ml water

2 cloves garlic

5 ml black peppercorns

1 dried bay leaf

2 whole cloves

Red vegetables

Red peppers, deseeded and sliced

Cooked beetroots, peeled and sliced

Red onions, sliced

Red cherry tomatoes

Red cabbage, sliced

Aubergines, sliced into long fingers

Green vegetables

Cucumber, sliced or chopped

Green peppers, deseeded and sliced

Courgettes, cut into ribbons

Green beans

Mange tout

Fennel bulb, quartered

Yellow vegetables

Onions, cut into wedges

Yellow patty pans, quartered

Yellow peppers, deseeded and sliced

Baby corn

Yellow cherry tomatoes

Gooseberries

Makes: *3x 500 g jars*

Difficulty: *Easy*

Prep time: *30 min + overnight chilling*

Cooking time: *5 min*

Serve with cheese, bread, cold meats and a glass of very drinkable red.

METHOD

For the pickling liquid, heat the sugar, vinegar, water, garlic and preferred spices in a saucepan over low heat, stirring occasionally until the sugar has dissolved. Set aside to cool slightly.

Place all the red vegetables in one sterilised jar, the yellow vegetables in another, and the green veg in a third jar, pour in enough pickling liquid to cover the vegetables and leave in the fridge overnight. Use within 3–4 days and store in the fridge.

*The pickling liquid is sufficient to fill one 500 g jar. Other herbs and spices you can use include Fresh rosemary, fresh thyme, fresh mint, dried chilli, coriander seeds, fennel seeds and mustard seeds.

BANANA AND SALTED CARAMEL POPCORN SMOOTHIE

Serves: *2*

Difficulty: *Easy*

Prep time: *20 min*

Cooking time: *15 min*

INGREDIENTS

Salted Caramel Popcorn

120 g popped popcorn

15 ml fine sea salt

200 g granulated sugar

250 g butter

125 ml golden syrup

Smoothie

3 frozen bananas, peeled and
   chopped

20 ml crunchy peanut butter or
   speculoos butter

250 ml plain yoghurt

METHOD

For the popcorn, line a tray with baking paper and grease with nonstick spray. Place the popcorn in a large bowl and season with the salt.

Heat the sugar, butter and syrup in a saucepan over medium-low heat. Cook, stirring occasionally, for 5 minutes, or until the sugar has dissolved. Bring the mixture to the boil and cook, without stirring, for another 5–8 minutes, or until golden. Remove from the heat and pour over the popcorn. Stir until coated. Spread onto the prepared tray and set aside to cool.

For the smoothie, blitz the frozen bananas, peanut butter, yoghurt and salted caramel popcorn together until combined. Don't make it too fine; you still want to bite into popcorn.

Note: Peel the bananas before freezing; they're actually easier to peel from the other tip instead of the stem end.

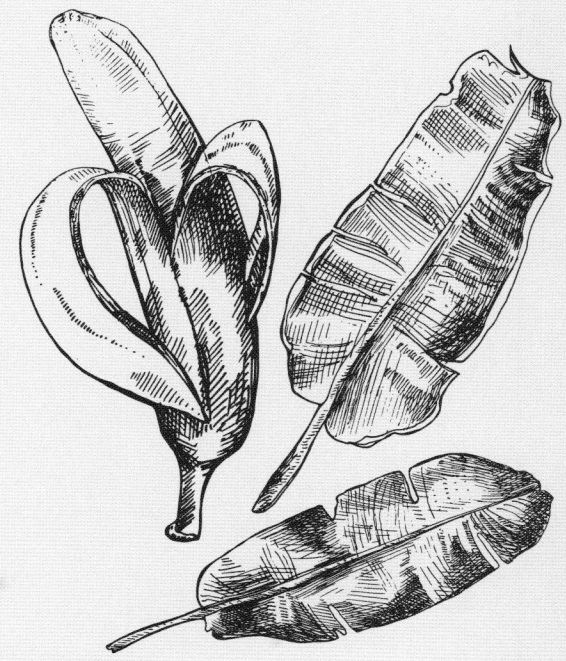

CREAMY SCRAMBLED EGGS

Serves: *1*
Difficulty: *Easy*
Prep time: *10 min*
Cooking time: *2 min*

Who needs a recipe for scrambled eggs is what you're thinking, right? Well, for perfect, creamy, fluffy eggs cooked to perfection there are a few pointers you need to know. Most important of these is: don't just use any eggs. I always use organic eggs. This is seriously one of those investments you need to make to take your scrambled eggs to a different level.

INGREDIENTS

2 large organic eggs
1 ml fine sea salt
Pinch ground black pepper
5 ml unsalted butter
50 ml crème fraîche
2.5 ml chopped chives
Flaky sea salt for serving

METHOD

Make sure you have all the ingredients ready before you start. Crack the eggs into a medium-sized bowl and add the fine salt and black pepper. Use a whisk to whip the eggs for about 30 seconds until pale yellow in colour.

Melt the butter in a medium-sized nonstick pan over medium-low heat and add the eggs when the butter starts to foam. Leave the eggs undisturbed until a thick layer of cooked egg forms around the edge of the pan. Use a rubber spatula and big movements and push the eggs all the way around the circumference of the pan, then across the base. Add the crème fraîche and chives and continue stirring until the eggs are barely setting. This should take about 2 minutes. The secret is that they should still look runny on top. Immediately place on a warm plate and sprinkle with a few more pinches of chopped chives and sea salt flakes.

DUKKAH AVOCADO TOAST

GIFT IDEA

Serves: *1*
Difficulty: *Easy*
Prep time: *15 min*
Cooking time: *5 min*

The dukkah gets made in large quantities beforehand and can be stored in an airtight container for up to one month. As part of my after-service ritual, I take a Cape seed loaf home and toast it before I top it generously with sliced avocado and the spice mix. Add to that an ice-cold beer and Netflix and it's the perfect way to end the day!

INGREDIENTS

Dukkah

150 g hazelnuts

65 g sesame seeds

30 g cumin seeds

20 g coriander seeds

20 g fennel seeds

5 ml ground cinnamon

10 ml dried mint

5 ml fine sea salt

Ground black pepper

Avocado Toast

1 ripe avocado, sliced

2 slices Cape Seed Loaf (see
*   page 24), toasted*

Extra virgin olive oil

Squeeze fresh lemon juice

Few pinches fresh parsley or your
*   favourite herb*

Red onion, very thinly sliced

METHOD

Measure all the ingredients for the dukkah separately. Use a large pan and place over medium heat. Toast the nuts and each of the seeds separately as they will toast differently due to their sizes. Give the pan a shake now and then to make sure they toast evenly. Place the mix in a food processor with the cinnamon, mint, salt and pepper and blend until the desired consistency is reached. I like mine with a bit of grain just to keep me awake while eating it late, late at night.

Arrange the avocado on each slice of toasted bread. Top with some dukkah and then drizzle with olive oil and lemon juice. Top with fresh herbs and red onion slices.

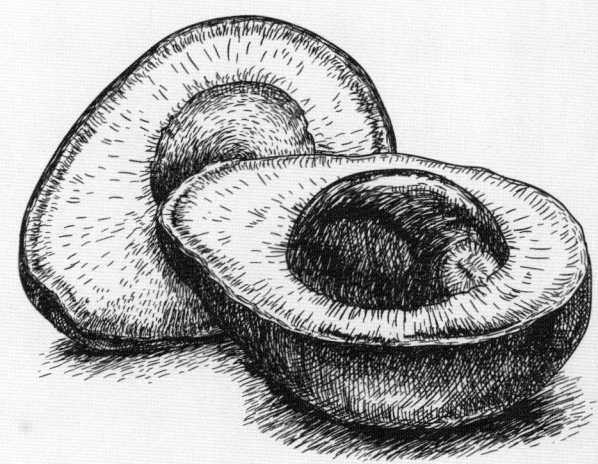

BILTONG AND
CRISP SANDWICH

Serves: *2*

Difficulty: *Easy*

Preparation time: *5 min*

Cooking time: *0 min*

Don't judge a sandwich by its filling. Over the years this has become a snack I admittedly enjoy so much that I actually get tears in my eyes when I eat it. Until now, this has been a closely guarded secret.

INGREDIENTS

4 slices soft, fresh white bread (or Pain de Mie, see page 32)

30 ml Mrs Ball's chutney

30 ml Mayonnaise (see page 248)

Thinly sliced biltong, wet or dry, to your preference

Chutney flavoured crinkle-cut crisps

METHOD

Place the slices of bread side by side. Spread chutney over two of the slices and mayonnaise over the remaining two slices. Arrange the biltong and crisps on the chutney slices and top with the mayo slices. And enjoy!

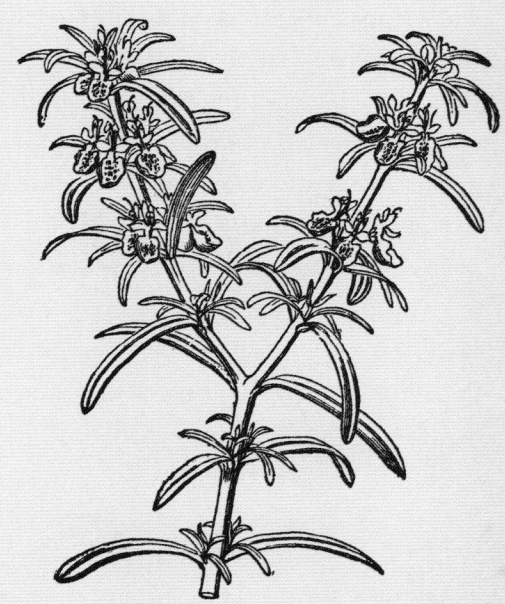

PANCAKES WITH MUSHROOMS AND GRUYÈRE

Serves: *2*

Difficulty: *Easy*

Prep time: *15 min + 1 hr resting for batter + 30 min infusing*

Cooking time: *20 min*

INGREDIENTS

Pancakes

3 eggs

1 egg yolk

30 ml granulated sugar

35 ml butter, melted

1 vanilla pod, split lengthways

500 ml milk

220 g all-purpose flour

30 ml sunflower oil for frying

Béchamel Sauce

250 ml milk

½ onion studded with 2 whole cloves

1 dried bay leaf

30 ml butter

15 ml all-purpose flour

30 g Gruyère cheese, grated

Sea salt and ground black pepper

Mushrooms

400 g exotic mushrooms or whichever kind you have

50 g butter

4 sprigs fresh thyme, leaves picked

METHOD

Make the pancakes first. Mix the eggs, egg yolk, sugar and melted butter in a small bowl. Scrape the vanilla seeds into the milk, add the vanilla pod and place over low heat until heated through. Sift the flour into a large jug, make a well in the centre and pour in the egg and butter mixture. Add the warm milk and mix until the batter is free of lumps. Rest the batter for at least 1 hour or store it in the fridge for the next day.

Heat a frying pan and add a drizzle of oil. Add a ladleful of batter and tilt the pan to spread it evenly. Cook for about 1 minute over medium heat until the bottom is golden. Flip and cook the other side for a minute. Remove the pancake from the pan and keep warm. Repeat with the rest of the batter, or keep the batter in the fridge for up to two days. The batter makes 10–15 pancakes.

For the béchamel, heat the milk, studded onion and bay leaf until just simmering. Remove from the heat and set aside to infuse for 30 minutes. Discard the studded onion and bay leaf. Heat butter in a saucepan until melted. Add the flour and fry the roux until golden. Whisk in the milk and cook for 5 minutes, or until the sauce has thickened and the flour has cooked out. Add the cheese and season well. Place a piece of plastic wrap onto the surface to prevent a skin from forming.

For the mushrooms, heat a large pan over high heat. Add the mushrooms and dry-fry until golden and all the moisture has evaporated. Add the butter and thyme and season well with salt and pepper.

To serve, divide the mushrooms and some shaved Gruyère between two pancakes, fold over and pour the béchamel over the top. Top with extra shaved Gruyère.

12.

MISE EN PLACE

[mi zɑ̃ ˈplas] – a French culinary phrase that means
'putting in place' or preparing ingredients, sauces,
vegetables or any items during a shift

*This chapter brings together all the extra sauces and condiments used
throughout the book.*

MAYONNAISE

Makes: *500 ml*
Difficulty: *Easy*
Prep time: *15 min*
Cooking time: *0 min*

2 egg yolks
5 ml lemon juice
2.5 ml Dijon mustard
375 ml canola oil
5 ml salt and pinch white pepper

Place the yolks, lemon juice and Dijon mustard in the bowl of a food processor. With the processor running, slowly stream in the canola oil and continue blending until the mayonnaise is fully emulsified. Season with salt and white pepper. Store in the fridge for two to three days.

SHALLOT CONFIT

Makes: *375 ml*
Difficulty: *Easy*
Prep time: *10 min*
Cooking time: *2 hr*

750 ml olive oil
2 cloves garlic
8 medium-sized shallots, peeled
2 sprigs fresh thyme
5 ml fine salt

Preheat the oven to 180 °C. Combine all the ingredients in a small ovenproof dish and cover with foil. Cook the shallots in the oven until they are tender and can easily be pierced with a fork. This will take around 1 hour 45 minutes to 2 hours. Store the shallots in their oil and seasonings in a jar in the fridge for two to three days.

PASTA DOUGH

Makes: *500 g*
Difficulty: *Little effort*
Prep time: *20 min +*
    30 min chilling
Cooking time: *5 min*

5 ml saffron
450 g Italian-style '00' flour
9 egg yolks
5 ml fine salt

Bring 250 ml water and the saffron to a boil in a small saucepan and reduce to 60 ml liquid. Strain. Place the flour on a stainless steel or marble worktop and make a well in the centre. Pour 12.5 ml of the saffron water, the egg yolks and salt into the well. Using a fork and working from the centre of the well, incorporate the flour into the wet ingredients. Once together, knead for 10 minutes until the dough is somewhat elastic. Depending on the humidity you may need to add more flour. Wrap in plastic wrap and refrigerate for 30 minutes before using.

CHICKEN STOCK

Makes: *4 L*
Difficulty: *Easy*
Prep time: *20 min*
Cooking time: about *3 hr*

5 kg chicken carcasses, including
    necks, wings and backs
7 kg ice cubes
220 g leeks, chopped
140 g celery, diced
140 g carrots, diced
140 g shallots, diced
140 g fennel, diced
1 dried bay leaf
1 sprig fresh thyme
2 whole cloves
10 black peppercorns

Rinse the bones well under running water. Place the bones in a large stock pot and top with the ice. Bring to a simmer over medium heat. Skim all the impurities and fats off the top while it simmers. After skimming, add the rest of the ingredients. Simmer uncovered for 3 hours, skimming every 30 minutes. Strain before use. Store in the fridge for up to three days or freeze for up to two months.

FISH STOCK

Makes: *1 L*
Difficulty: *Easy*
Prep time: *20 min*
Cooking time: *30 min*

15 ml vegetable oil
2 medium-sized onions, sliced
4 stalks celery, sliced
2 medium-sized carrots, peeled and sliced
2.5 kg fish heads and bones, rinsed clean of blood and chopped
1 kg lobster heads or prawn shells
250 ml dry white wine
2 dried bay leaves
Large handful fresh parsley
6 sprigs fresh thyme
15 ml black peppercorns

Heat the oil in a large stockpot over medium heat. Sauté the onions, celery and carrots until soft and translucent. Add the fish heads and bones and the lobster heads or prawn shells, pour wine over and cover the pot tightly. Leave to sweat for 10–15 minutes. Add enough water to just cover the bones. Tie the bay leaves, parsley and thyme together with kitchen string. Add the herbs and black peppercorns and bring to a simmer.

Skim the foam off using a ladle; be careful not to remove any of the spices or herbs. Simmer for 20 minutes. Strain out the vegetables and bones and pour through a muslin cloth. Cool completely before covering. The stock will keep for up to three days in the fridge or can be frozen for two months.

ROASTED VEGETABLES

Fresh vegetables. Firm, juicy and packed with flavour. Make sure to cut them the same size so that they roast evenly. Starchy vegetables such as potatoes and pumpkin can be undercooked, so make sure the cut is not too big. Roast smaller vegetables whole. They don't only taste great, but they also look beautiful. Cauliflower can be sliced in thick whole slices and broccoli can just be cut in half. Use a good olive oil to moisten the veg well. If you roast vegetables that suck up the oil, keep them moist throughout the roasting period, but be careful that you don't overdo it as the last thing you want is to have them turn out greasy. Don't be shy to use enough seasoning. This will help develop the flavour during the cooking process. Use a baking tray (rather than a roasting pan with high sides) and make sure there is enough space between the vegetables so that when they give off steam they don't become mushy. Heat up that oven! I like to go up to 220 °C and toss the veg well during the roasting time, otherwise you will have one side dark and one side lighter. The average roasting time is 35–40 minutes.

BROWN BEEF STOCK

Makes: *2–3 L*
Difficulty: *Easy*
Prep time: *20 min*
Cooking time: *about 4 hr*

2.5 kg beef stock bones
15 ml vegetable oil
4 carrots, peeled and sliced
4 stalks celery, sliced
2 onions, halved
60 ml tomato paste
500 ml red wine
Large handful fresh parsley
8 sprigs fresh thyme
2 dried bay leaves
1 head garlic, halved
5 ml black peppercorns

This stock will keep for up to five days in the fridge or can be frozen for up to three months.

Preheat the oven to 220 °C. Place the beef bones on an oven tray and roast for 25–30 minutes until browned, turning occasionally.

Heat the oil in a large stockpot over medium-high heat. Add the carrots, celery and onions and sauté until golden brown. Reduce heat to medium, add the tomato paste and fry for 4–5 minutes, or until the acidity is cooked out. Deglaze the pot with the red wine and cook for 5–10 minutes, or until all the alcohol is cooked out. Tie the parsley, thyme and bay leaves together with kitchen string. Add the herbs, garlic and black peppercorns to the pot.

Cover with 2 L water and bring to a simmer for 3–4 hours, occasionally skimming off the foam and fat. Add more water when needed. Strain out the vegetables and bones and pour through a muslin cloth. Cool completely before covering.

THE JAN VINAIGRETTE

Makes: *250 ml*
Difficulty: *Easy*
Prep time: *10 min*
Cooking time: *0 min*

30 ml honey
15 ml Dijon mustard
125 ml raspberry vinegar
Sea salt and ground black pepper
Juice of ½ lemon
250 ml grapeseed oil or sunflower oil

Friday at lunchtime is a busy time for us: deliveries come in on a big scale, we prep for a full house and we get ready for dinner at the same time. A tuna salad with fresh endives, nuts and seeds — or basically anything we can lay our hands on — goes onto a large platter drizzled with the secret ingredient we all know will bring it together… Sonja's vinaigrette. She uses a blender without a lid (apparently she has more control), but I don't recommend you try this at home as she has ended up with a vinaigrette facial on numerous occasions.

You can also use a glass bottle with a lid and give it a few good shakes. The vinaigrette can be stored in the fridge for up to 2 weeks.

Mix all the ingredients, except the oil, in a blender. Mix on slow speed, then slowly add the oil until the consistency reaches a creamy dressing.

SUN-DRIED TOMATO JAM

GIFT IDEA

Makes: *1 jar*
Difficulty: *Easy*
Prep time: *10 min*
Cooking time: *30 min*

30 ml olive oil

240 g sun-dried tomatoes, sliced

2 shallots, thinly sliced

1 clove garlic, minced

30 ml honey

60 ml red wine vinegar

125 ml Chicken Stock (see
   page 249)

180 ml water

5 ml dried thyme

Sea salt and ground black pepper

Warm the olive oil and gently fry the tomatoes and shallots for about 5 minutes until softened. Stir in the garlic, cook for about 1 minute and then add the honey, vinegar, chicken stock, water, thyme, salt and pepper. Stir well and bring to a boil. Reduce heat to low and simmer for about 30 minutes until most of the liquid has reduced. Remove from the heat, pour into a blender, pulse quickly a few times and pour into a bowl if using straight away, or into a sterilised jar if making ahead (it will keep in the fridge for up to six weeks).

CARROT PURÉE

Makes: *500 ml*
Difficulty: *Easy*
Prep time: *15 min*
Cooking time: *35 min*

180 g butter

12 medium-sized carrots, peeled
   and thinly sliced

15 ml fine salt

1 L water

Melt the butter in a medium-sized saucepan over medium heat. Add the carrots and salt and sweat for 5 minutes. Add the water, cover the saucepan and cook until the carrots are very tender — this will take anything from 20 to 30 minutes. Strain, reserving the liquid.

Purée the carrots in a blender until smooth, adding a little of the reserved cooking liquid if necessary to blend. Push through a fine-mesh sieve until silky smooth.

PARSNIP PURÉE

Makes: *500 ml*
Difficulty: *Easy*
Prep time: *15 min*
Cooking time: *15 min*

125 g butter
1 kg parsnips, peeled and diced
375 ml water
250 ml fresh cream
5 ml fine salt

Melt the butter in a medium-sized saucepan over medium heat. Add the parsnips and sweat until they start to break down. Add the water and cover. Continue to cook until the parsnips are tender. Drain and purée in a blender while adding the cream. Season with salt.

GINGER GEL

Makes: *250–300 ml*
Difficulty: *Medium*
Prep time: *15 min*
Cooking time: *35 min*

Simple syrup
200 g sugar
250 ml water

Ginger gel
3 large pieces fresh ginger, peeled
   and cut into pieces
10.5 g agar agar

Make the simple syrup first. Combine the sugar and water in a small saucepan over medium heat. Heat until the sugar has melted. Cool and store in the fridge until ready to use. (Use within two weeks.)

In a small saucepan, bring the simple syrup and the ginger to a simmer and cook slowly for 30 minutes. Strain the syrup though muslin cloth or a fine-mesh sieve into a separate saucepan.

Combine the agar agar with the syrup and set over medium to high heat. Whisk continuously for 5 minutes. Once the agar agar is completely dissolved, pour the mixture into a baking dish and refrigerate for 1 hour. Once set, cut into small pieces and purée in a blender until smooth. Pass through a fine-mesh sieve before using. Store in a squeeze bottle in the fridge for up to one week.

VARIATIONS
Lemon gel: Substitute the fresh ginger with 500 ml freshly squeezed lemon juice.
Berry gel: Substitute the fresh ginger with 500 ml berry purée.
Red wine gel: Substitute the fresh ginger with 750 ml red wine and reduce the liquid to 500 ml.

INDEX

Aïoli 119
Almonds
  Fig rocky road 199
  Roast lamb with stuffed
    pumpkin flowers 109
  Roasted butternut and
    almond quiche 88
Anchovies
  Pissaladière 44
  Roast lamb with stuffed
    pumpkin flowers 109
  Roasted asparagus and
    leeks with anchovy and
    bacon 68
Apples
  Apple and cider charlotte 146
  Apple butter 62
  Salmon in a herb garden 125
Asparagus
  Roasted asparagus and
    leeks with anchovy and
    bacon 68
  Seared tuna with asparagus and
    whipped egg yolk 61
Avocado
  Dukkah avocado toast 237
  Grilled prawn with courgette
    flower, cucumber and
    avocado gazpacho 48
  Salmon in a herb garden 125

Bacon
  Everyone's favourite
    spaghetti bolognese 214
  Pork terrine with marinated
    vegetables 95
  Roasted asparagus and leeks
    with anchovy and bacon 68
  Souttert with sun-dried
    tomato jam and Charroux
    mustard 57
Baguettes 20
Bananas
  Banana and salted caramel
    popcorn smoothie 231
  Chocolate mousse cake with
    roasted banana 162
  Roasted banana, rum and raisin
    rice cake 224
Basil pesto 78
Beans
  French bean, grape and
    hazelnut salad with
    grapefruit 208
Beef see also Veal
  Brown beef stock 251
  Everyone's favourite
    spaghetti bolognese 214
  Pot-au-feu 211
  Roast beef fillet with chestnuts
    and mushrooms 106

Beetroot
  Salt-roasted beetroot and goat's
    cheese crêpes 73
  Slow-braised pork belly with
    beetroots 99
Berry gel 253
Biltong and crisp sandwich 240
Bread
  Baguettes 20
  Cape seed loaf 24
  Foccacia 218
  French white bread 27
  Levain starter dough 18
    Stiff 18
  Mosbolletjies 38
  Pain au chocolat 41
  Pain de mie 32
  Pain rustique 28
  Poolish starter dough 18
  Pretzels with Kalahari Desert
    salt 35
Butter
  Burnt butter, honey and buchu
    madeleines 180
  Homemade butter 142
  Whipped miso butter 137
Butternut
  Roasted butternut and
    almond quiche 88

Cabbage
  Pot-au-feu 211
Cake
  Chocolate mousse cake with
    roasted banana 162
  Crumbled carrot cake with
    orange curd and hazelnut
    ice cream 161
  Pear and white chocolate
    hazelnut cake 156
  Roasted banana, rum and raisin
    rice cake 224
  Camembert and cognac-soaked
    berry cake 134
Caramel 179
  Caramel and pistachio tuile 193
  Cider caramel 146
Carrots
  Carrot purée 252
  Crumbled carrot cake with
    orange curd and hazelnut
    ice cream 161
  Pot-au-feu 211
  Slow-braised pork belly with
    beetroots 99
  Vegetable bouillon with fresh
    herb ravioli 87
Cashew nuts
  Fig rocky road 199
Cassis berries
  Chocolate and cassis tart 168

Cauliflower
  Cod with corn, cauliflower and
    popcorn powder 131
  White chocolate and scallop
    ice cream with cauliflower
    purée and black rice
    chips 54
Cheese
  Baked Parmesan courgette
    fries 221
  Camembert and cognac-soaked
    berry cake 134
  Chicken liver and Parmesan
    mousse 92
  Fig and blue cheese mini
    tarte Tatins 47
  Homemade ricotta 141
  Lamb shank with Parmesan
    crumb crust 110
  Pancakes with mushrooms and
    Gruyère 243
  Poached pear and blood
    orange salad with goat's
    cheese 205
  Roast lamb with stuffed
    pumpkin flowers 109
  Roasted butternut and
    almond quiche 88
  Salt-roasted beetroot and goat's
    cheese crêpes 73
  Souttert with sun-dried
    tomato jam and Charroux
    mustard 57
  Tempura courgette flowers
    stuffed with zesty
    ricotta 202
  Tomato and crab salad with
    basil pesto 78
Cheesecake, Lemon and poppy
  seed 152
Cherries, Poached 92
Chestnuts
  Roast beef fillet with chestnuts
    and mushrooms 106
Chicken
  Chicken liver and Parmesan
    mousse 92
  Chicken stock 249
Chocolate
  Berries and chocolate 155
  Chocolate and cassis tart 168
  Chocolate bark 176
  Chocolate mousse 155
  Chocolate mousse cake with
    roasted banana 162
  Chocolate pistachio tuile 155
  Chocolate sponge 162
  Fig rocky road 199
  Naartjie panna cotta with
    white chocolate rocks 190
  Pain au chocolat 41

Pear and white chocolate
  hazelnut cake 156
Tiramisu 171
White chocolate and scallop
  ice cream with cauliflower
  purée and black rice
  chips 54
Cider caramel 146
Coconut
  Fig rocky road 199
  Naartjie panna cotta with
    white chocolate rocks 190
  Salmon in a herb garden 125
Cod with corn, cauliflower and
  popcorn powder 131
Coffee
  Coffee and vodka salmon
    gravlax with egg yolk
    cream 122
  Tiramisu 171
Corn
  Cod with corn, cauliflower and
    popcorn powder 131
Courgettes
  Baked Parmesan courgette
    fries 221
  Grilled prawn with courgette
    flower, cucumber and
    avocado gazpacho 48
  Tempura courgette flowers
    stuffed with zesty
    ricotta 202
Crab
  Tomato and crab salad with
    basil pesto 78
Crêpes, Savoury buckwheat 73
Croissants see Pain au chocolat
Cucumber
  Grilled prawn with courgette
    flower, cucumber and
    avocado gazpacho 48

Desserts
  Apple and cider charlotte 146
  Berries and chocolate 155
  Chocolate and cassis tart 168
  Chocolate mousse cake with
    roasted banana 162
  Crumbled carrot cake with
    orange curd and hazelnut
    ice cream 161
  Lemon and poppy seed
    cheesecake 152
  Melon and orange granita 172
  Milk tart croquembouche 179
  Milk tart with poached
    fruit 149
  Naartjie panna cotta with
    white chocolate rocks 190
  Pear and white chocolate
    hazelnut cake 156

Roasted banana, rum and raisin rice cake 224
Spicy pear saffron tarte Tatin 165
Tiramisu 171
Duck
Magret de canard with tonka jus 103
Dukkah 237

Eggs
Coffee and vodka salmon gravlax with egg yolk cream 122
Creamy scrambled eggs 234
Mayonnaise 248
Seared tuna with asparagus and whipped egg yolk 61
Souttert with sun-dried tomato jam and Charroux mustard 57
Endives
Glazed endive, spelt and caramelised sunflower seed salad 82

Fennel
Bourride 119
Lamb shank with Parmesan crumb crust 110
Salmon in a herb garden 125
Figs
Fig and blue cheese mini tarte Tatins 47
Fig rocky road 199
Pork chops with whiskey-soaked figs 217
Fish and seafood
Baked trout provençale 128
Bourride 119
Cod with corn, cauliflower and popcorn powder 131
Coffee and vodka salmon gravlax with egg yolk cream 122
Fish stock 250
Grilled prawn with courgette flower, cucumber and avocado gazpacho 48
Salmon in a herb garden 125
Seared scallops with lemony salsa verde 116
Seared tuna with asparagus and whipped egg yolk 61
Stuffed sardines with lemon and roasted onions 115
Tomato filled with haddock and a light apple butter, dusted with popcorn powder 62
White chocolate and scallop ice cream with cauliflower purée and black rice chips 54
Flax seeds
Cape seed loaf 24
Foccacia 218
Foie gras
Veal cheeks cooked in red wine with foie gras 100
Fruit pastels 196

Gels
Berry gel 253
Ginger gel 253
Lemon gel 253
Red wine gel 253
Ginger
Ginger gel 253
Grilled prawn with courgette flower, cucumber and avocado gazpacho 48
Slow-braised pork belly with beetroots 99
Grapefruit
French bean, grape and hazelnut salad with grapefruit 208
Grapes
French bean, grape and hazelnut salad with grapefruit 208

Haddock
Tomato filled with haddock and a light apple butter, dusted with popcorn powder 62
Hazelnuts
Crumbled carrot cake with orange curd and hazelnut ice cream 161
Fig rocky road 199
French bean, grape and hazelnut salad with grapefruit 208
Pear and white chocolate hazelnut cake 156
Honey
Burnt butter, honey and buchu madeleines 180
Cape seed loaf 24
Glazed endive, spelt and caramelised sunflower seed salad 82
Magret de canard with tonka jus 103
Slow-braised pork belly with beetroots 99

Ice cream see also Sorbet
Crumbled carrot cake with orange curd and hazelnut ice cream 161
White chocolate and scallop ice cream with cauliflower purée and black rice chips 54

Jam, Sun-dried tomato 252

Lamb
Lamb shank with Parmesan crumb crust 110
Roast lamb with stuffed pumpkin flowers 109
Leeks
Bourride 119
Pot-au-feu 211
Roasted asparagus and leeks with anchovy and bacon 68
Slow-braised pork belly with beetroots 99

Vegetable bouillon with fresh herb ravioli 87
Lemons
Lemon and poppy seed cheesecake 152
Lemon gel 253
Seared scallops with lemony salsa verde 116
Stuffed sardines with lemon and roasted onions 115
Tempura courgette flowers stuffed with zesty ricotta 202
Lettuce
Glazed endive, spelt and caramelised sunflower seed salad 82
Levain starter dough 18
Stiff 18
Limes
Salmon in a herb garden 125

Madeleines, Burnt butter, honey and buchu 180
Magret de canard with tonka jus 103
Malva truffles with smoked rosemary 184
Marinated vegetables 95
Mayonnaise 248
Aïoli 119
Melon and orange granita 172
Meringues
Raspberry and cream meringue kisses 187
Milk tart
Milk tart croquembouche 179
Milk tart with poached fruit 149
Mosbolletjies 38
Mushrooms
Pancakes with mushrooms and Gruyère 243
Roast beef fillet with chestnuts and mushrooms 106
Vegetable bouillon with fresh herb ravioli 87
Mustard
Souttert with sun-dried tomato jam and Charroux mustard 57

Naartjie panna cotta with white chocolate rocks 190

Olives
Baked trout provençale 128
Olive and rosemary sticks with whipped miso butter 137
Pissaladière 44
Onions see also Spring onions, Shallots
Pissaladière 44
Poached pear and blood orange salad with goat's cheese 205
Oranges
Crumbled carrot cake with orange curd and hazelnut ice cream 161

Golden shallot and orange custard 74
Melon and orange granita 172
Poached pear and blood orange salad with goat's cheese 205

Pain de mie 32
Pain rustique 28
Pancakes see also Crêpes
Pancakes with mushrooms and Gruyère 243
Socca 51
Parsley
Seared scallops with lemony salsa verde 116
Vegetable bouillon with fresh herb ravioli 87
Parsnip purée 253
Pasta
Everyone's favourite spaghetti bolognese 214
Pasta dough 249
Vegetable bouillon with fresh herb ravioli 87
Pastry
Camembert and cognac-soaked berry cake 134
Fig and blue cheese mini tarte Tatins 47
Olive and rosemary sticks with whipped miso butter 137
Pastry puffs 179
Spicy pear saffron tarte Tatin 165
Sweet pastry 149
Pears
Muscat-poached pears and quinces 149
Pear and white chocolate hazelnut cake 156
Poached pear and blood orange salad with goat's cheese 205
Spicy pear saffron tarte Tatin 165
Peas
Glazed endive, spelt and caramelised sunflower seed salad 82
Pesto, Basil 78
Pine nuts
Basil pesto 78
Salt-roasted beetroot and goat's cheese crêpes 73
Pineapple
Slow-braised pork belly with beetroots 99
Pissaladière 44
Pistachios
Caramel and pistachio tuile 193
Chocolate pistachio tuile 155
Pork terrine with marinated vegetables 95
Poolish starter dough 18
Popcorn
Popcorn powder 131
Salted caramel popcorn 231
Poppy seeds
Cape seed loaf 24
Lemon and poppy seed cheesecake 152

Pork
Pork chops with whiskey-
soaked figs 217
Pork terrine with marinated
vegetables 95
Slow-braised pork belly with
beetroots 99
Prawns
Bourride 119
Grilled prawn with courgette
flower, cucumber and
avocado gazpacho 48
Pretzels with Kalahari Desert
salt 35
Pumpkin
Roast lamb with stuffed
pumpkin flowers 109
Purées
Carrot purée 252
Cauliflower purée 54
Parsnip purée 253

Quiche, Roasted butternut
and almond 88
Quinces
Muscat-poached pears and
quinces 149

Raisins
Poached pear and blood orange
salad with goat's cheese 205
Roasted banana, rum and
raisin rice cake 224
Raspberry and cream meringue
kisses 187
Red pepper
Baked trout provençale 128
Rice
Roasted banana, rum and
raisin rice cake 224
White chocolate and scallop ice
cream with cauliflower purée
and black rice chips 54
Ricotta, Homemade 141

Salads
French bean, grape and
hazelnut salad with
grapefruit 208

Glazed endive, spelt and
caramelised sunflower
seed salad 82
Poached pear and blood orange
salad with goat's cheese 205
Red, green and yellow
pickled salad 228
The JAN vinaigrette 251
Tomato and crab salad with
basil pesto 78
Salmon
Coffee and vodka salmon
gravlax with egg yolk
cream 122
Salmon in a herb garden 125
Sardines
Stuffed sardines with lemon
and roasted onions 115
Sauces
Béchamel 243
Caramel 179
Cider caramel 146
Raspberry cream 187
Yoghurt vanilla cream 155
Scallops
Seared scallops with lemony
salsa verde 116
White chocolate and scallop
ice cream with cauliflower
purée and black rice
chips 54
Sesame seeds
Cape seed loaf 24
Dukkah 237
Shallots
Golden shallot and orange
custard 74
Pork terrine with marinated
vegetables 95
Seared scallops with lemony
salsa verde 116
Shallot confit 248
Vegetable bouillon with fresh
herb ravioli 87
Smoothie, Banana and salted
caramel popcorn 231
Socca 51
Sorbet
Roasted banana sorbet 162

Soup and broth
Grilled prawn with courgette
flower, cucumber and
avocado gazpacho 48
Vegetable bouillon with fresh
herb ravioli 87
Spelt
Glazed endive, spelt and
caramelised sunflower
seed salad 82
Spring onions
Stuffed sardines with lemon
and roasted onions 115
Stocks
Brown beef stock 251
Chicken stock 249
Fish stock 250
Strawberries
Berries and chocolate 155
Sunflower seeds
Glazed endive, spelt and
caramelised sunflower
seed salad 82

Tarts (savoury)
Fig and blue cheese mini
tarte Tatins 47
Souttert with sun-dried
tomato jam and Charroux
mustard 57
Tarts (sweet)
Chocolate and cassis tart 168
Milk tart with poached
fruit 149
Spicy pear saffron tarte
Tatin 165
Tempura courgette flowers
stuffed with zesty
ricotta 202
Terrine
Pork terrine with marinated
vegetables 95
Tomatoes
Baked trout provençale 128
Bourride 119
Everyone's favourite
spaghetti bolognese 214
Lamb shank with Parmesan
crumb crust 110

Sun-dried tomato jam 252
Tomato and crab salad with
basil pesto 78
Tomato filled with haddock
and a light apple butter,
dusted with popcorn
powder 62
Tonka beans
Magret de canard with
tonka jus 103
Trout
Baked trout provençale 128
Truffles
Malva truffles with smoked
rosemary 184
Tuiles
Caramel and pistachio
tuile 193
Chocolate pistachio tuile 155
Tuna
Seared tuna with asparagus and
whipped egg yolk 61
Turnips
Pot-au-feu 211

Vanilla sponge 171
Veal
Veal cheeks cooked in red wine
with foie gras 100
Vegetables, Roasted 250
Vinaigrette, The JAN 251

Walnuts
Crumbled carrot cake with
orange curd and hazelnut
ice cream 161

Yoghurt
Banana and salted caramel
popcorn smoothie 231
Grilled prawn with courgette
flower, cucumber and
avocado gazpacho 48
Yoghurt vanilla cream 155

Published in 2016 by Struik Lifestyle
(an imprint of Penguin Random House South Africa (Pty) Ltd)
Company Reg. No. 1953/000441/07
The Estuaries, 4 Oxbow Crescent, Century Avenue, Century
City, 7441
P O Box 1144, Cape Town 8000, South Africa
www.randomstruik.co.za

Copyright © in published edition:
Penguin Random House South Africa (Pty) Ltd 2016
Copyright © in text: Jan Hendrik van der Westhuizen 2016
Copyright © in illustrations: As credited below
Copyright © in photographs: Jan Hendrik van der Westhuizen 2016

All illustrations from www.shutterstock.com, except
pp. 5, 9, 67 and 113 (www.vintageprintable.com).
Cover is a collage of imagery from www.shutterstock.com,
www.vintageprintable.com and *Graphic Frames* by the
Pepin Press & Agile Rabbit Editions.

Reprinted in 2016 (twice), 2017 (twice)

Publisher: Linda de Villiers
Managing editor: Cecilia Barfield
Editor and indexer: Joy Clack
Concept Designer: Fred Viljoen
Designer: Beverley Dodd
Photographer and stylist: Jan Hendrik van der Westhuizen
Proofreader: Glynne Newlands

Reproduction by Hirt & Carter Cape (Pty) Ltd
Printed and bound by RR Donnelley Asia
Printing Solutions Ltd

ISBN 978 1 43230 608 3

MIX
Paper from
responsible sources
FSC® C101537

From the same author

The French Affair
ISBN 978 1 43230 197 2

Fig. 12.

12.ᶜ

14.ᵈ